THE STORY OF THE
RUGBY
WORLD
CUP
SOUTH
AFRICA
1995

ROYSTON & LAMOND

INTERNATIONAL

THE OFFICIAL BOOK
OF THE SOUTH AFRICAN
RUGBY FOOTBALL UNION FOR
THE RUGBY WORLD CUP
SOUTH AFRICA 1995
·
ENDORSED BY THE
SOUTH AFRICAN
GOVERNMENT
THROUGH THE OFFICE OF
THE MINISTER OF SPORT
AND RECREATION

Joost van der Westhuisen breaks from the pack in the tense opening game of the 1995 Rugby World Cup at Newlands

THE GAME BEGINS

Let us recall the myth:
During a game of football, played on The Close at Rugby School in the midlands of England in 1823, a pupil was overwhelmed by a flash of inspiration, like Paul on the Damascus road. He took up the ball in his hands and ran with it. And, lo, all who saw it were filled with wonder and said: "That is how we want to play." To confirm this miraculous occurrence, there is a stone tablet set into the wall at the close.

Students at Rugby School re-enact the game that changed their rules forever.

Now let us review the facts: In 1823, William Webb Ellis was only fourteen, pretty low down on society's hierarchical tree and hardly important enough to be considered a great innovator. Nobody had yet heard the word, soccer, for neither the game, nor the name, had come into being.

There was no overriding body to say who could play what, where, when and how. Rules of football changed from match to match and place to place.

In English schools, rules were adapted to the available ground. Various schools played various games with varying laws, but alumni wanted to keep on playing and needed the game to be regulated.

In 1863 a Football Association was formed to draw up a set of rules governing play. One such rule was that players were forbidden to touch the ball with their hands. This was the birth of soccer.

Blackheath, most of whose members were Old Rugbyeans, led a breakaway to form the Football Union and decided to adopt the rules of their old school. Hence the Rugby Football Union.

So what did Ellis do? And why the myth?

He may have caught the ball for a free kick, and instead of moving back, as was common practice, ran forward with it.

The tablet was set in 1893, seventy years after Ellis ran the ball.

The plaque in the old brick wall at Rugby School which bears the inscription:

THIS STONE COMMEMORATES THE EXPLOITS OF WILLIAM WEBB ELLIS WHO WITH FINE DISREGARD FOR THE RULES OF FOOTBALL AS PLAYED IN HIS TIME, FIRST TOOK THE BALL IN HIS HANDS AND RAN WITH IT THUS ORIGINATING THE DISTINCT FEATURE OF THE RUGBY GAME A.D. 1823

French fullback, Jean-Luc Sadourny on the burst during the 1995 Five Nations match against Ireland.

The myth may have been an act of snobbery, to emphasise how the origins of the game came from the inspiration of a fine public school boy on the green playing fields of England, and not from the saturnine souls of avaricious miners in the bowels of the earth wanting compensation for playing the game.

Fact or fiction, in the history of rugby the name of William Webb Ellis will be forever famous.

The game transferred easily from England to foreign soils, in the main through British subjects who went out into the world, expanding their own fortunes along with the wealth of the realm of Queen Victoria's British Empire.

In the home counties, rugby had gone from the school to the universities, then further afield, as graduates spread the game as teachers and army officers. These men became rugby's earliest missionaries, whose acolytes were to be found wherever there were gatherings of physically active men. And that is how the game spread - to the schools, universities, army units and the mines, which is why in South Africa, Kimberley was such a powerful centre in the early days.

The influence of these early advocates for the game tended to make rugby the preferred game for society's upper crust; the preserve of men from public schools, a class of men most likely to be able to afford to play the game for the game's sake.

But as the game grew in popularity in other countries, the nature and personality of its adherents became more varied. In Ireland it was used as a means of reconciliation between the Catholic south and the Protestant north. In South Africa, too, rapprochement between the battling Boers and Brits after the Anglo-Boer War was a motivating factor. In Wales and New Zealand the game captured the imagination of all classes of society and, even today, they are the most egalitarian of rugby's adherents.

Englishmen took the game to Paris where it caught on rapidly, especially among the Basques of the south-west. The French, in turn, introduced the game to the rest of Europe - to Romania and Italy in particular - and to Francophone Africa.

The game reached the Americas via the British in Canada and an elitist bastion of amateurism was established in Argentina. Missionaries from New Zealand took the game to the Pacific islands and it filtered from the British outposts of Hong Kong and Singapore through the Far East, especially Japan.

The Rugby World Cup suggests a world game, which rugby is. The fastest growing team game in the world.

The Queen (who is amused) presents the trophy to Nick Farr-Jones (who is thrilled!) when Australia defeated England 12-6 to win the gold Webb Ellis trophy and the title of 1991 Rugby World Cup Champions.

Serge Blanco the try maker, the captain, the hero, the legend of France.

THE BIRTH OF THE RUGBY WORLD CUP

Rugby people are a conservative breed. Change happens slowly. As far back as 1904 there was a suggestion that injured players be replaced, but the RFU threw it out as being contrary to the "Spirit of our Game". It took over sixty years for it to become law. Eighty years later there was objection to a Rugby World Cup as well.

The prime movers behind the first Rugby World Cup were Australia and New Zealand. England, Scotland and Ireland opposed the idea. South Africa's vote was crucial on the eight-member committee. South Africa voted in favour and so it came to pass.

Australia and New Zealand thought it would be good for the game. The Australians were especially enthusiastic because in their country the game lagged behind Rugby League and Australian Rules. The Southern Hemisphere had no equivalent to the Five Nations Championship.

The organisers were given some eighteen months to do the job. Sponsors were difficult to get, though the Japanese company, KDD, stepped into the breech.

The first World Cup was an instant success. It was fun, there was an opportunity for individual players to achieve international reknown, and there was the chance for the game to make money. It was not long before big business became involved.

From the start the Rugby World Cup has been a business - run by Rugby World Cup Limited, a wholly owned subsidiary of the International Rugby Football Board. It organises the World Cup for teams of both 15 and 7 a-side. It must also collect money for the use of the 67 countries that are now members of the IRFB.

The directors of Rugby World Cup Limited are Sir Ewart Bell of Ireland (chairman) , Marcel Martin of France, Keith Rowlands of Wales, Leo Williams of Australia, Nic Labuschagne of South Africa and Colin Jones of Barclays on the Isle of Man.

It is a business, and as such, must be profitable in order to ensure the growth of rugby as a world game. The World Cup in South Africa has achieved both outcomes.

England captain Will Carling in action during the 1991 World Cup final at Twickenham.

THE FIRST RUGBY WORLD CUP: 1987

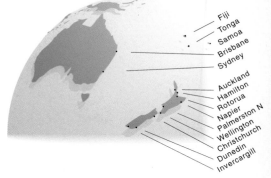

Fiji
Tonga
Samoa
Brisbane
Sydney

Auckland
Hamilton
Rotorua
Napier
Palmerston N
Wellington
Christchurch
Dunedin
Invercargill

Rugby, at last, leapt onto the world stage with the first Rugby World Cup. Suddenly it was a megasport commanding attention in the media and kindling great interest beyond its traditional adherents. Rugby changed in 1987, and it will never be the same again.

The first tournament was a massively successful marketing exercise for rugby, strengthening the game against threats from other sports and attracting a new generation to its fold, not only players and spectators but also people with money. The Rugby World Cup was a profitable venture.

It changed the game for three reasons.

Firstly, the money would rush the game headlong towards professionalism. Players would have to produce more and as a result would want more. The demands of the game would preclude normal career development, and rugby would therefore have to provide and do so generously.

The old-world amateurs in England, Scotland and Ireland had seen this clearly but the tournament proved so enjoyable and successful that any voice of protest was drowned in the general excitement. The best the traditionalists could do was to try to hang onto the brakes as the vehicle raced towards money.

Secondly, the Rugby World Cup was so high profile that countries would now plan from World Cup to World Cup. Many intervening internationals would not be the do-or-die matches of yesteryear; they would be part of a build-up to the next tournament. One would seldom see the report of a match without mention of the next World Cup.

The All Blacks were responsible for the third change. They were streets ahead of the rest of the world on the field; so much better that they jolted everybody out of their complacency and a new style of rugby developed, aping the All Blacks. It was a more physical, more calculating game, played at close quarters, sharply attacking the advantage line.

The results reveal the story as they smashed all opposition, including France in a one-sided final. It was New Zealand all the way.

1987 RUGBY WORLD CUP		
22/5	Auckland	New Zealand 70 - Italy 6
23/5	Sydney	Australia 19 - England 6
23/5	Auckland	Romania 21 - Zimbabwe 20
23/5	Christchurch	France 20 - Scotland 20
24/5	Hamilton	Fiji 28 - Argentina 9
24/5	Brisbane	USA 21 - Japan 18
24/5	Napier	Canada 37 - Tonga 4
25/5	Wellington	Wales 13 - Ireland 6
27/5	Christchurch	New Zealand 74 - Fiji 13
28/5	Wellington	France 55 - Romania 12
28/5	Christchurch	Argentina 25 - Italy 16
29/5	Palmerston	Wales 29 - Tonga 16
30/5	Wellington	Scotland 60 - Zimbabwe 21
30/5	Sydney	England 60 - Japan 7
30/5	Dunedin	Ireland 46 - Canada 19
31/5	Brisbane	Australia 47 - USA 12
31/5	Dunedin	Italy 18 - Fiji 15
1/6	Wellington	New Zealand 46 - Argentina 15
2/6	Auckland	France 70 - Zimbabwe 12
2/6	Dunedin	Scotland 55 - Romania 28
3/6	Invercargill	Wales 40 - Canada 9
3/6	Brisbane	Ireland 32 - Tonga 9
4/6	Sydney	England 34 - USA 6
4/6	Sydney	Australia 42 - Japan 23
QUARTER FINAL:		
6/6	Christchurch	New Zealand 30 - Scotland 3
7/6	Auckland	France 31 - Fiji 16
7/6	Sydney	Australia 33 - Ireland 15
8/6	Brisbane	Wales 16 - England 3
SEMI FINAL:		
13/6	Sydney	France 30 - Australia 24
14/6	Brisbane	New Zealand 49 - Wales 6
PLAY-OFF		
18/6	Rotorua	Wales 23 - Australia 21
FINAL:		
20/6	Auckland	New Zealand 29 - France 9

Black-eyed but a deep sense of satisfaction for David Kirk knowing he and his golden boys in All Black jerseys are number one: the first ever Rugby World Cup Champions.

THE SECOND RUGBY WORLD CUP: 1991

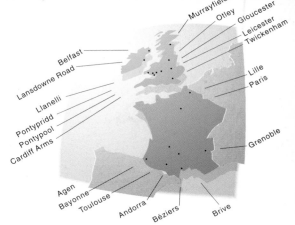

I f the overriding memory of the 1987 World Cup was of one team, the mighty All Blacks, it was another Antipodean team that caught the imagination in 1991 and, more conspicuously there was an individual.

Australia won the Rugby World Cup, deservedly and refreshingly, but without dominating as the All Blacks had in 1987. Some of the matches were heart-stoppingly close. The Wallabies were within moments of losing to Ireland in the thrilling quarter final in Dublin. Neither were they convincing against England at Twickenham in the final. But then closeness and might-have-beens add spice to sport. Their conduct was a credit to the game. They were the wholesome face of rugby football.

Yet the team which caught the imagination and the hearts of the public and commentators in 1991 was the side from tiny Western Samoa, making its debut in the World Cup. They had qualified in the Asian-Pacific Group by beating Korea, Tonga and Japan. They came to the World Cup quietly. Soon people sat up and took notice. Their captain, from Auckland, the piano-mover Peter Fatialofa, became one of the personalities of the tournament. Western Samoa beat Wales in Cardiff, and the world was astounded. They lost by three penalty goals to one in a titanic clash with the Wallabies in the wet of Pontypool and they ended by smashing Argentina in Pontypridd. They made the quarter finals and, when they lost 28 - 6 to Scotland, much of the romance went out of the World Cup.

The star player of the tournament, possibly rugby's brightest star ever, was David Campese. There were many great players at the World Cup that year - Tim Horan and Jason Little, Michael Lynagh and Nick Farr-Jones, John Kirwan, John Jeffrey of Scotland, Fatialofa and Frank Bunce of Western Samoa, Ivan Farncescato of Italy, Yoshito Yoshida of Japan, Simon Poidevin, Peter Winterbottom, and Willie Ofahengaue, and more. But none shone the way 'Campo' did - his telling, powerful try against the All Blacks in the semi-final, his delicate flip over his shoulder to send Tim Horan in for a try; David Campese was everything that was best in the derring-do of rugby.

Australia's world record points scorer, Michael Lynagh, along with a star studed team, helped clinch the 1991 Rugby World Cup

1991 RUGBY WORLD CUP

Date	Venue	Result
3/10	Twickenham	New Zealand 18 - England 12
4/10	Llanelli	Australia 32 - Argentina 19
4/10	Béziers	France 30 - Romania 3
5/10	Otley	Italy 30 - USA 9
5/10	Murrayfield	Scotland 47 - Japan 9
5/10	Bayonne	Canada 13 - Fiji 3
6/10	Dublin	Ireland 55 - Zimbabwe 11
6/10	Cardiff	W. Samoa 16 - Wales 13
8/10	Gloucester	New Zealand 46 - USA 6
8/10	Twickenham	England 36 - Italy 6
8/10	Grenoble	France 33 - Fiji 9
9/10	Murrayfield	Scotland 51 - Zimbabwe 12
9/10	Dublin	Ireland 32 - Japan 16
9/10	Pontypool	Australia 9 - W. Samoa 3
9/10	Cardiff	Wales 16 - Argentina 7
9/10	Toulouse	Canada 19 - Romania 11
11/10	Twickenham	England 37 - USA 9
12/10	Murrayfield	Scotland 24 - Ireland 15
12/10	Cardiff	Australia 38 - Wales 3
12/10	Brive	Romania 17 - Fiji 15
13/10	Leicester	New Zealand 31 - Italy 21
13/10	Pontypridd	W. Samoa 35 - Argentina 12
13/10	Agen	France 19 - Canada 13
16/10	Belfast	Japan 52 - Zimbabwe 8
QUARTER FINAL:		
19/10	Murrayfield	Scotland 28 - W. Samoa 6
19/10	Paris	England 19 - France 10
20/10	Dublin	Australia 19 - Ireland 18
20/10	Lille	New Zealand 29 - Canada 13
SEMI FINAL:		
26/10	Murrayfield	England 9 - Scotland 6
27/10	Dublin	Australia 16 - New Zealand 6
PLAY-OFF		
30/10	Cardiff	New Zealand 13 - Scotland 6
FINAL:		
2/11	Twickenham	Australia 12 - England 6

THE ROAD TO
SOUTH AFRICA

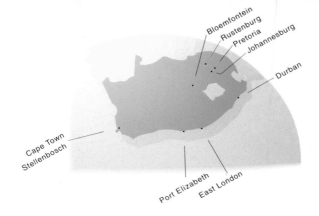

Bloemfontein
Rustenburg
Pretoria
Johannesburg
Durban
Cape Town
Stellenbosch
Port Elizabeth
East London

Nine countries were automatic qualifiers for the 1995 Rugby World Cup - the eight that played in the 1991 quarter-finals (Australia, England, New Zealand, Scotland, Ireland, Western Samoa, France and Canada) and South Africa, the host country. All other countries, including Wales, had to qualify.

To find the other qualifiers, the world was divided into zones: Europe, The Americas, Africa, Asia and the Pacific Rim. Europe was allowed three qualifying teams, the others one each.

The 1995 Rugby World Cup began in Andorra in October 1992. In that first match Andorra beat Denmark 3-0. Altogether 51 countries took part. There would have been 52 but Luxembourg could not find sufficient funds and was unable to fulfil its first fixture against Andorra.

A great many teams played in Europe where FIRA (the Rugby Federation started by France on the lines of FIFA in soccer) did much to spread the game. This zone had by far the most teams. Eventually the favoured nations won through, seeing off the likes of Portugal and Spain. The final seeding and the order was Wales, Italy and Romania.

The Americas zone ended in a contest between Argentina and the USA Eagles which the Pumas won.

To qualify, Fiji and Tonga fought it out. Tonga won in Fiji and Fiji won in Tonga, but Tonga had a better points difference, and so qualified.

There were two qualifying rounds for the African zone, one held in Tunis and one in Nairobi, before the deciders were played in Casablanca. The participants were Zimbabwe, Namibia, Morocco and Ivory Coast. Namibia were expected to walk it. They walked all right. They walked right out as Ivory Coast shocked the rugby world by becoming Africa's qualifiers.

The Asians were the last to qualify by way of a tournament in Kuala Lumpur, Malaysia. That became the occasion for a world record when Hong Kong beat Singapore 164-13. There were thirteen matches in the tournament. The winners scored 816 points, the losers 118. The decider always looked to be between Korea and Japan. Japan won 26-11 and qualified.

England captain, Will Carling, in action during the 1995 Five Nations match against Ireland.

The 52 countries that contested the right to participate in the third Rugby World Cup.	
Andorra	Lithuania
Argentina	Luxembourg
Australia	Malaysia
Belgium	Morocco
Bermuda	Namibia
Canada	New Zealand
Chile	Paraguay
Czech Rep.	Poland
Denmark	Portugal
England	Rep.of China
Fiji	Russia
France	Scotland
Georgia	Singapore
Germany	South Africa
Gulf States	Spain
Holland	Sri Lanka
Hong Kong	Sweden
Hungary	Switzerland
Ireland	Thailand
Israel	Tonga
Italy	Tunisia
Ivory Coast	Uruguay
Japan	USA
Kenya	Wales
Korea	W. Samoa
Latvia	Zimbabwe

SOUTH AFRICA

In no country in the world do people expect success on the rugby field with greater intensity than in South Africa, but then no country in the world has equalled South Africa's achievements.

The country has won more tests against all opposition than it has lost. The lead has shrunk since getting back into world rugby in 1992, but it is still ahead. It was the first country to beat New Zealand in New Zealand - back in 1937. The next team to do so was the Lions of 1971. The Springboks achieved four successive grand slams on tours to the UK and Ireland, a feat New Zealand and Australia have performed once each.

Isolation resulting from apartheid began to bite in the early Seventies and, after a brief respite in the early Eighties, became nearly complete. During isolation South Africa played provincial rugby with a passion, and a myth took hold that this kept its rugby so strong that it could still take on, and beat, the rest of the world.

This was an illusion. The divisiveness of provincial rugby had weakened, rather than strengthened, the national side. The rest of the world now had a way of playing which was foreign to South Africans who still believed, with delightful naiveté, that the game could be played from first phase possession, and that it was about avoiding a tackle, not taking one.

For all that, there is talent and determination aplenty among the country's rugby players; enough to enable it to become the second country to win the Rugby World Cup on its debut. New Zealand did it in 1987 and after this year, no country will have a realistic chance of doing it again.

There are facilities and administrative capabilities enough this year for the Rugby World Cup to be played in a single country for the first time ever. And there is speed and strength and skill enough among the players for the trophy to stay in South Africa for the next four years.

SQUAD

Francois Pienaar - Captain

Gavin Johnson	Ruben Kruger
Andre Joubert	Robby Brink
Pieter Hendriks	Mark Andrews
James Small	Kobus Wiese
Brendan Venter	Hannes Strydom
Japie Mulder	Krynauw Otto
Christian Scholtz	Pieter Du Randt
Joel Stransky	Balie Swart
Hennie Le Roux	Marius Hurter
Joost Van der Westhuizen	Garry Pagel
Johan Roux	James Dalton
Rudolf Straeuli	Chris Rossouw
Adriaan Richter	

TEAM MANAGEMENT

Morne Du Plessis	Manager
Kitch Christie	Coach
Gysie Pienaar	Assistant Coach
Dr F Verster	Doctor
Evan Speechly	Physiotherapist

South African Rugby Football Union was founded in 1889. Only recently has the game become available in a unified form to all South Africans. In a population of 40 million, 1004 clubs field 78 000 players.

Balance, poise, grace. South Africa's fly half, Joel Stransky kicks for goal.

AUSTRALIA

They are the champions. The world's finest will not find it easy to topple them.

New Zealand became world champions in 1987, and the Wallabies took the crown away from them with an emphatic 16-6 victory in the quarter-final in Dublin in 1991. Nobody then, nor since, would gainsay their right to call themselves the Champions of the World. Their results have justified the title and, more to the point, is the manner in which they have played the game.

The strength of Australian rugby is in the east - New South Wales, Queensland and the Australian Capital Territory - and even there the code plays second fiddle to rugby league. In the South and West, Australian Rules dominates. But the union game has had a solid foundation in many of the schools, especially the great public schools of which St. Joseph's College in Sydney is the most famous.

In the past, prestige and the opportunity to earn large sums of money in the rugby league has meant that rugby union players in Australia have tended to be young, and the game was largely confined to eager, slightly naive, very athletic university students.

That is changing. Players still go across to league, but at a slower rate. The structures of Australian rugby have allowed for greater sophistication. Players have retained their athleticism but have taken it many levels higher. They have taken the skills of the game and refined them, adding resilience to the mix. And then there has been the rise of rugby in Queensland, the product of excellent administration, where today they are arguably the strongest provincial team in the world of rugby football.

Despite the careful attention to detail, Australia's new approach to rugby, which began in the days of the Ella brothers, is the most imaginative in the world and the most disciplined. Whereas in the past they had a team with some stars, they now have a team of all-stars, and one of them, David Campese, was the brightest at the 1991 Rugby World Cup. The star of the 1995 tournament could well come from the Wallaby ranks again.

SQUAD	
Michael Lynagh - Captain	
Scott Bowen	Phillip Kearns
Matthew Burke	Jason Little
David Campese	Roderick McCall
Troy Coker	Ewen McKenzie
Daniel Crowley	Willie Ofahengaue
Anthony Daly	Matthew Pini
John Eales	Joseph Roff
Michael Foley	Peter Slattery
Timothy Gavin	Damian Smith
George Gregan	Ilie Tabua
Mark Hartill	Warwick Waugh
Daniel Herbert	David Wilson
Timothy Horan	

TEAM MANAGEMENT	
Peter Falk	Manager
Bob Dwyer	Coach
Bob Templeton	Assistant Coach
John Best	Doctor
Greg Craig	Physiotherapist

South of the Murrumbidgee it is Aussie Rules Football, but north, into NSW, ACT and Queensland, rugby union holds sway behind rugby league. Australian Rugby Football Union was founded in 1949. The country currently produces 11 500 players in 350 clubs from the total population of 16 million.

World points record holder, and Australian captain, Michael Lynagh evades a tackle.

CANADA

They are big, enthusiastic, brave and ambitious - the rugby men of Canada.

There are no greater rugby enthusiasts than the Canadians. No country has greater ambitions or is confronted with such logistical problems. And no country has the travelling bills that the Canadians have.

Their star forward, Al Charron, lives in Ottawa in Canada's east. Most of the players come from the climatically more hospitable west in the beautiful province of British Columbia. Charron flies for seven hours to get to practice!

The players, as a whole, are possibly the greatest globe-trotters in the world, having played in nine foreign countries in the five months before coming to South Africa. Wisely so, as the domestic rugby of Canada is not enough to prepare players for the giant leap into competition with the Wallabies and the Springboks, who are in their pool.

The Canadians have men who are big and physical, but they find it hard to cope with the speed and skill of the modern game. They were bigger than the All Black pack in 1995 but were shoved around Eden Park and thrashed in the line-outs. Their older players found getting to the break-down an ordeal.

Their game, like that of the Romanians, is based on big forwards who are well organised in the set pieces and content to play a fairly static form of rugby.

Having opted for a more dynamic rucking game, they got to the quarter-finals of the 1991 World Cup before they lost at Lille in the north of France, not without honour, to the All Blacks.

Ian Birtwell, the Englishman who has done so much for the development of Canada's national team, has tried a more expansive approach, but the intuition for such a form of rugby is not really there for men who tend to take up the game late in life.

Their biggest ambition is to be recognised amongst the top nations of the rugby world. Canada supports its rugby players and its long term challenge must be to encourage younger men to turn out bearing the proud maple leaf on their chests. For this season, experience and courage will have to do the job.

S Q U A D	
Gareth Rees - Captain	
Richard Bice	Rod Snow
Mark Cardinal	Karl Svoboda
Al Charron	John Graf
Glenn Ennis	Steve Gray
Eddie Evans	David Lougheed
Ian Gordon	Shawn Lytton
John Hutchinson	Bob Ross
Mike James	Winston Stanley
Paul LeBlanc	Christian Stewart
Gordon MacKinnon	Alan Tynan
Colin McKenzie	Scott Stewart
Chris Michaluk	Ron Toews
Gareth Rowlands	

T E A M M A N A G E M E N T	
Ray Skett	Manager
Ian Birtwell	Coach
Rod Holloway	Assistant Coach
Mike Bassett	Doctor
Jane Drouln	Physiotherapist

Canadian Rugby Union was founded in 1929 and reformed in 1965. With its harsh winters and national predominance with ice-hockey, Canada's 25 million population still manages to produce 11 670 players from 220 clubs.

Al Charron, Canada's bustling eighth man looks for support on a typical drive.

ROMANIA

Romania is a country whose people have gone through tough times, and its rugby has suffered as a result. It suffered because of corruption in the previous government. It suffered in the uprising that ousted Nicholas Ceausescau, when players were killed, including Florica Murariu, the national captain. And it has suffered even in the freedom that followed the revolution.

Freedom meant mobility. Many of the players left the struggling country for a better life, especially in France which, from the beginning, has been Romanian rugby's godfather. The depleted ranks of those who stayed suffered from the Seine drain. Romanian rugby has always depended on the bravery that is best produced by team spirit and the ability to make a little go a long way; the first casualty of the exodus was team spirit.

Unlike the Canadians, Romania changed its policy for the World Cup - to sacrifice experience for youth. It wanted its team to rediscover national pride and attract the young players; the country's rugby future.

Despite France's patronage, Romanian rugby has none of the romance and flair of the French. Their rugby is more like that of Canada and Russia; based on stern forwards able to manufacture set-piece ball which the fly-half has, with dutiful dullness, ballooned downfield.

This policy, combined with the heat and austerity of Bucharest has, in the past, brought it victory over Wales and Scotland and, most pleasingly, France, beaten in 1990 in Paris. The French, who kept Romania in international rugby, paid their visitors the compliment of playing its best team. Joy knew no bounds.

Touring has been tough for the Romanians, because of a lack of funds. On a trip to Ireland they were found stranded without money for food for themselves and the crew of the aircraft which they had chartered, and for fuel for the plane journey home. The Irish helped out. The rugby world also helped raise funds for the reconstruction of the country's rugby after the revolution.

There is a long and brave road ahead for the Romanians who love the game with a passion.

SQUAD

Tiberiu Brinza - Captain

Gheorge Leonte	Gheorghe Solomie
Ionel Negreci	Vasile Brici
Leodor Danut Costea	Gabriel Vlad
Constantin Cojocariu	Valere Tufa
Sandu Ciorascu	Andrei Branescu
Alexandru Gealapu	Ovidiu Slusariuc
Traian Oroian	Vasile Mugurel
Eugen Branza Tiberiu	Ilie Ivanciuc
Daniel Neaga	Vasile Ioan Lucaci
Neculai Nichitean	Sebastian Draguceanu
Ionel Rotaru	Catalin Fugigi
Nicolae Racean	Adrian Lungu
Romeo Gotineac	Lucian Ioan

TEAM MANAGEMENT

Teodor Radulescu	Manager
Mircea Paraschiv	Coach
Constantin Fugigi	Assistant Coach
Liviu Cariadi	Doctor

Federati Romania de Rugbi was established in 1913. Of the 22 million population, 20 000 players have emerged to play for 98 clubs.

Determination is etched on the face of the Romanian backs as they look to break the line.

ENGLAND

he game of rugby football is in England's debt - at least on two counts: it owes its existence to England and, more importantly it gave rugby football the priceless legacy of sportsmanship which is so under threat today from the tyranny of profit.

For years it was England that determined the laws and even the manner in which the game was played. The sport was governed with a rod of iron and, significantly, there was far less scandal in the game then than there is these days when the individual is supreme.

England has the most registered players in the world and the oldest playing traditions. This in a country that cherishes tradition and pomp. A visit to Twickenham has, for rugby followers, the same air of pilgrimage as a visit to Westminster Abbey for others.

As happens with much of man's endeavours, age brings decline. So it is with rugby football. England too has lost much of the spirit of adventure, the good manners of the past and the innocent belief that the game should be played for its own sake. Its rugby, too, has developed a commercial soul.

To be more competitive financially, rugby in England has been brilliantly marketed. Its followers, the wealthiest in the world of rugby football, have made of the sport a great occasion. The game has lost its edge of generosity and friendliness. Playing in leagues, week after week for points, has undoubtedly brought a more competitive edge to English rugby. Since their introduction in 1986 the game in England has been galvanised, particularly at international level. England have been transformed from a hit and miss outfit into one of the leading powers in the modern game.

Historically, England has not been consistent. During the same year they both beat the All Blacks and lost to Ireland. The next year they beat the Springboks and again lost to Ireland. But more and more they look capable of consistency and the discipline needed to take them to the top.

S Q U A D	
Will Carling - Captain	
Neil Back	Richard West
Martin Bayfield	Rob Andrew
Ben Clarke	Kyran Bracken
Graham Dawe	Jonathan Callard
Martin Johnson	Mike Catt
Jason Leonard	Phil de Glanville
John Mallett	Jeremy Guscott
Brian Moore	Damian Hopley
Steve Ojomoh	Ian Hunter
Dean Richards	Dewi Morris
Tim Rodber	Rory Underwood
Graham Rowntree	Tony Underwood
Victor Ubogu	

TEAM MANAGEMENT

Jack Rowell	Manager
John Elliot	Assistant Manager
Les Cusworth	Assistant Coach
Terry Crystal	Doctor
Kevin Murphy	Physiotherapist

Home of rugby, the Rugby Football Union was founded in 1871. Today England has 2 405 clubs and fields and 375 000 players from its total population of 47 million.

Rob Andrew, England's most capped fly half, executes a kick with assurance and style.

ARGENTINA

Argentinian rugby may be described as the best of games, and the worst of games. An honourable way of life, and a base form of insult. Uppercrust, and low as the gutter. The pastime of gentlemen, and the crude violence of thugs. Friendly and hostile. Splendid, and basically ugly.

The clubs where rugby is played in Argentina are the most magnificent in the world of rugby football. They are the big, spacious, gracious clubs of the world's wealthy. They have as members the men who can afford to be amateur, and nowhere in the world is the amateur principle adhered to more fiercely than in Argentina. Even advertising is viewed with suspicion. But then, paradoxically, amateurism makes it the game of the elite.

Argentinians are passionate about rugby football, but more so about the amateur principle. For this reason, they have lost some of their best players who have sought reward for their efforts in less altruistic Italy.

Their passion at times spills over into unacceptable behaviour on the field. But they have learnt that what happens on the field, stays on the field; what happens off the field remains for life. And so they will hug and kiss after a tough match and celebrate until the early hours of the morning.

They think and plan a great deal, and have come up with the idea that the scrum is the most important facet of the game. Using engineering principles, they devised the *bajada* scrum that is certainly the most cohesive of any in the world. But their play beyond that is confined almost entirely to kicking and charging. While their inclination is free-spirited, their style seems to run along regimented lines.

Their rugby did produce one of the all-time greats of the game - Hugo Porta. They have, in the past, had famous victories, though most of them have been close to home. In two World Cups they have won one match, which is anomalous as there is a great deal of talent in the land of the Pampa and the gaucho.

S Q U A D	
Sebastian Salvat - captain	
Lisandro Arbizu	German Llanes
Diego Albanese	Rolando Martin
Nicolas Bossicovich	Federico Mendez
Pablo Buabse	Jose Luis Cilley
Martin Corral	Ernesto Noriega
Rodrigo Crexell	Agustin Pichot
Diego Silva	Jose Santamarina
Fernando Del Castillo	Pedro Sporleder
Guillermo Del Castillo	Martin Sugasti
Francisco Garcia	Martin Teran
Sebastian Irazoqui	Marcelo Urbano
Ezequiel Jurado	Cristian Viel
Ricardo Le Port	

TEAM MANAGEMENT	
Luis Chauleu	Manager
Alejandro Petra	Coach
Ricardo Paganini	Coach
Dr. Mario Larrain	Doctor

The game of the elite, Union Argentina de Rugby was founded in 1899 and currently has 16 500 players in 188 clubs from the total population of 24 million.

Speed and elusiveness among the Argentinian backs is typical of the country's game.

WESTERN SAMOA

In 1991 Western Samoa astounded the rugby world. They came to the World Cup for the first time and made it through to the quarter-finals by beating Wales.

The world was delighted - not because they beat Wales but because their success implied that rugby was indeed a world game. Nobody had seen them as a threat - just another team to make up the numbers. But they had forgotten that the men from Samoa often played in New Zealand. Many have followed in the footsteps of Bryan Williams and gone on to become All Blacks, players like Michael Jones, Frank Bunce, the Bachop brothers, Va'iaga Tuigamala and Alama Ieremia. The world forgot this at their peril, and it was Wales' fate to be highjacked in Cardiff.

Success at the 1991 World Cup was a two-edged sword for the Samoans. On the one hand it brought them glory. The whole of the rugby world wanted to play them, in contrast to the ribald laughter that had greeted Danie Craven not long before the tournament when he suggested that Western Samoa be invited to tour South Africa. Playing around the world brought money to Western Samoan rugby.

On the other hand, fame also meant that players were snapped up elsewhere. Apart from those who made it as All Blacks, some, like Apollo Perelini and Lolani Koko, went off to rugby league.

Their rugby is brave and fast. They are the roughest tacklers in the world, more zealous than judicious at times, and they get around the field at speed to do so. Their aggressive defence often produces for them the possession which they are denied at primary sources, and they have flair and inventiveness to turn possession into triumph.

Why Western Samoa? The western side of the volcanic islands of Samoa was administered by New Zealand which introduced rugby football. The eastern part was administered by the USA and the sportsmen learnt gridiron. Pita Fatialofa, one of the world's most popular rugby men, believes many gridiron players would greatly strengthen Manu Samoa's rugby.

S Q U A D	
Pita Fatialofa - Captain	
Tala Leiasameivao	Tu Nuualiitia
Brendan Reily	Vaa Vitale
George Laui	Darren Kellet
Mike Mika	Khera Puleitu
Darryl Williams	Fereti Tuilagi
Lio Falarriko	Feta Sini
Potu Leevasa	To'o Vaega
Saini Lemanea	George Leaupepe
Pat Lam	Brian Lima
Malaki Lupeli	George Harder
Junior Paramore	Mika Umaga
Sila Viafale	Tupo Faamaino
Shem Tatupu	

TEAM MANAGEMENT	
LT Simi	Manager
SP Schuster	Coach
BG Williams	Technical Advisor
Dr LS Ainuu	Doctor
Karen Sutton	Physiotherapist

Western Samoan Rugby Football Union was first formed in 1929. The tiny population of 156 000 produces 4 400 players in 91 clubs. After a bruising encounter, one opponent said: "We were lucky we only had to play one half of the island."

It takes extra commitment and concentration to stop a Western Samoan in full stride.

ITALY

Italian rugby is beginning to show la bella figura: the grand exterior that is a sign of worth.

For many years the seductive lira was the siren call that attracted so many of the world's rugby players. They have found it rewarding and enjoyable, but not especially demanding. Many people warned the Italians that the number of estranieri were inhibiting the growth of their own rugby. How wrong they were!

Various estranieri, mainly from South Africa, New Zealand, Australia and Argentina, spread the rugby gospel in Italy's venerable towns. Coaches, mainly from France, taught the Italians that rugby football had a hard side, as well as glamour, and that the hard side contained undignified activities such as tackling. And they developed a programme for coaching and inspiring young men.

It has paid off. Italian rugby has a new resolve and a disciplined pattern of playing.

Part of its new resolve has come from development from within. There has also been a stiffening of the talent pool by way of Argentinean players who have come to Italy and qualified for the Azzurri, the Blues.

La bella figura is more than just an exterior. Although there are important clubs in Catania, Rome and L'Aquila, the game in Italy flourishes above all in the north. Sponsorship of clubs was a vogue in Italy long before it got to other countries and, in fact, it kept the game going despite small, if voluble, crowds.

Rugby in Italy, which had the dubious distinction of the support of Benito Mussolini, has also benefited from competition in FIRA. Last year Italy beat France A for the first time.

Italy is already able to compete with the top countries without embarrassment (unlike at the inaugural World Cup when New Zealand beat them 70-6, the very first match of the tournament.) There is optimism about the future.

The Italian game could be about to take off.

S Q U A D	
Massimo Cuttitta - Captain	
Orazio Arancio	Mark Giacheri
Massimo Bonomi	Francesco Mazzariol
Stefano Bordon	Carlo Orlandi
Massimiliano Capuzzoni	Pierpaolo Pedroni
Andrea Castellani	Marco Platania
Carlo Checchinato	Franco Properzi
Marcello Cuttitta	Massimo Ravazzolo
Mauro Dal Sie	Andrea Sgorlon
Diego Dominguez	Moreno Trevisiol
Roberto Favaro	Luigi Troiani
Ivan Francescato	Alessandro Troncon
Julien Gardner	Paolo Vaccari
Mario Gerosa	

T E A M M A N A G E M E N T	
Giancarlo Dondi	Manager
Georges Coste	Coach
Massimo Mascioletti	Assistant Coach
Felice di Domenica	Doctor
Giorgio Morvidoni	Physiotherapist

Federazione Italiana Rugby was established in 1928. From its present population of 53 million, Italy produces 15 200 players registered in 265 clubs playing mainly in the more sophisticated north.

Paolo Vaccari of Italy turns defence into attack near his own line.

NEW ZEALAND

Rugby football has been representative of New Zealand's finest achievements. Not the friendliness of its people, nor the majesty of its mountains, the tranquillity of its lakes and the calm sweep of its deep inlets have brought it anything like the recognition of its rugby deeds. Nothing absorbs the attention of its people the way rugby does.

With a fairly small population of just over 3 million, (far fewer than the 66 million sheep), the people are naturally homogenous and they have no greater national focus than rugby football.

There is a wholesome face to New Zealand rugby not readily found in any other country. The game is egalitarian, knowing neither social nor class barriers. Student, labourer, policeman and businessman - they are all in it together. Women play, referee, administer and get involved in many other ways. The country recognises only one form of royalty - the All Black.

There are few things that New Zealand rugby has not achieved. It was the first of the colonies to tour Europe, back in 1881, with an astonishing team of native born New Zealanders who played an astounding number of matches to earn enough money to pay the tour's costs.

A special characteristic of the All Black player is his impassivity. Watch him when he is hurt; there is no visible sign that he is in pain. Watch him when his side scores a try; there is no extravagant elation. Watch him when the opposition scores; there is no apparent disappointment. He gives nothing away. He is possessed of a frightening calm - a man who has a job to do, and does it.

The country's rugby warriors have scaled the sport's Everest and set up many records. One, in particular, that nobody will ever take away, is victory in the first Rugby World Cup. Significantly, this task was achieved in such a way that the game of rugby has not been the same since.

If there is one team that will not be underestimated by any other, it is the All Blacks.

SQUAD

Sean Fitzpatrick - Captain

Graeme Bachop	Robin Brooke
Frank Bunce	Zinzan Brooke
Simon Culhane	Olo Brown
Marc Ellis	Craig Dowd
Alama Ieremia	Paul Henderson
Walter Little	Norman Hewitt
Jonah Lomu	Ian Jones
Andrew Mehrtens	Jamie Joseph
Glen Osborne	Josh Kronfeld
Eric Rush	Blair Larsen
Ant Strachan	Richard Loe
Jeff Wilson	Kevin Schuler
Michael Brewer	

TEAM MANAGEMENT

Laurie Mains	Manager
Earle Kirton	Coach
Ross Cooper	Assistant Coach:
Dr Michael Bowen	Doctor:
Barry Donaldson	Physiotherapist:

New Zealand Rugby Union was established in 1892. Three million citizens. One thousand clubs. One hundred and eighty two thousand five hundred players. With these figures its easy to see that everybody on the island is affected by the game.

New Zealand's total commitment to the game is never more illustrated than in the rucks and mauls.

IRELAND

"All their wars are happy and all their songs are sad," Gilbert Keith Chesterton said of the Irish, and it sums up the perverseness of the nation and its rugby.

For many years rugby was for the Irish a foreign sport, not to be touched by any lover of the true spirit of the Gaels. But the country has taken rugby to its heart. It plays the game with the warlike intensity of commandos and finds delight and joy in doing so. And in that battle against the mighty powers of the rugby world, little Ireland, for the only time in its troubled history, unites. Rugby football is all that brings together the north and the south. Ireland is Ireland on the rugby field - nowhere else.

This unifying spirit of joyous madness has made the Irish capable of the greatest feats - like toppling the grandiose might of England in three successive years with its hit-and-run tactics, and coming within moments of ejecting Australia from the 1991 World Cup.

What a day that was at Lansdowne Road, the oldest international ground still in use. Ireland broke the Australian grip and smashed its way out of defence on a raid that led to Gordon Hamilton's try which Ralph Keyes converted to give Ireland the lead. The whole nation began rejoicing. The Liffey would bubble with Guinness on that joyous night.

Then they missed touch from the kick-off and the Wallabies counter-attacked coolly in the midst of wild emotion, and eventually Michael Lynagh sliced over for the winning try in the corner in the midst of the saddest silence in the world.

And later the Liffey bubbled with Guinness in any case. Sure, it's not worth crying about. Didn't we give the Australians an awful shock and isn't Michael Joseph Lynagh an Irishman after all?

They can beat the good ones and lose to the bad ones, but they will enjoy what they do in any case. They are the game's amateurs after all. In today's professional climate, it becomes increasingly difficult for amateurs to produce the unexpected surprise that is sport's most delectable sauce.

SQUAD

Terry Kingston - Captain

Jim Staples	John Fitzgerald
Conor O'Shea	Keith Wood
Richard Wallace	Gary Halpin
Brendan Mullin	Paul Wallace
Jonathan Bell	David Tweed
Maurice Kiklo	Neil Francis
Simon Geogheoan	Gabriel Fulcher
Darach O'Mahony	Anthony Foley
Paul Burke	Denis McBride
Eric Elwood	Eddie Halvey
Niall Hogan	David Corkery
Michael Bradley	Paddy Johns
Nick Popplewell	

TEAM MANAGEMENT

Noel Murphy	Manager
Gerry Murphy	Coach
Dr Mick Murphy	Doctor

Irish Rugby Football Union was established in 1874. Ireland's population of nearly 5 million has 12 500 players fielded from 65 clubs.

Simon Geoghegan takes a bead on the loose ball in the match against the All Blacks.

WALES

The wonderful world of Welsh rugby preserves the spirit of druid ancestors, taking men from the dark bowels of the earth into the green daylight of heroic deeds; from the mine to the rugby field.

Only the French have something of the romantic expressiveness of the Welsh when talking about the game that has gone so to the heart of Welsh-ness.

Wales occupies a similar geographic area as the Kruger National Park, and the strength of its rugby comes from only a small region of that country - stretching roughly from Newport in the east, seventy miles to Llanelli in the west and some fifteen miles inland to Neath and Pontypool - a small sliver of land that has produced some of the greatest rugby geniuses of all time, all of whom have passed immediately into legend as folk heroes. The Principality has its own royalty, most of them rugby players - men like Cliff Morgan and his entire magic generation: Barry John, Gareth Edwards, JPR Williams, Gerald Davies, JJ Williams, Phil Bennett, Mervyn Davies and more. What a miracle Wales gave to rugby football!

The game in Wales has been an expression of the Welsh spirit - an egalitarian game where everybody from Dai University to Dai Mine has an equal voice, and no fear of using it. The rugby club is the social centre of the town, an escape from the terraced houses into spacious rooms; with the chance of bumping into one of those who perform heroic feats on the open green field.

The great generation also gave Wales a feeling of equality with the rest of the world. No longer was the country a conquered land, forced to serve the wealthy in the east. No longer was it a nation of dunces forced to speak a foreigner's language. Rugby football gave Wales national pride, and it set about the game with lilting fervour; above all at Cardiff Arms Park, the ground with a legendary spirit of heroism. Make it at the Arms Park, boyo, and you can make it anywhere.

The possibility of heroic deeds is never far from Welsh rugby.

SQUAD

Mike Hall - Captain

Tony Clement	Stuart Davies
Adrian Davies	Richard Evans
D Evans	Michael Griffiths
Ieuan Evans	J Humphreys
S Ford	Gavin Jenkins
Neil Jenkins	S John
Robert Jones	Derwyn Jones
Andy Moore	Emyr Lewis
Wayne Proctor	Gareth Llewellyn
Gareth Thomas	G Prosser
J Thomas	Stuart Roy
M Bennett	Hemi Taylor
John Davies	

TEAM MANAGEMENT

Geoff Evans	Manager
Alex Evans	Coach
Mike Ruddock Dennis John	Assistant Coach
Roger Evans	Doctor
Mark Davies Tudor Jones	Physiotherapist

Welsh Rugby Union was founded in 1880. From their 3 million population 40 000 Welshmen from 178 clubs play rugby.

Gareth Thomas has reason to smile as he runs in for another try.

JAPAN

For the Japanese, rugby football is a serious and honourable business. The country exports all manner of goods, but, like Italy, it imports rugby players - from Australia, New Zealand, the Pacific Islands and Canada. And some of those players have qualified to play for Japan, thus going some way to solving its main rugby problem - a lack of height.

They scrum well and race about the field bravely and inventively, but they struggle for real possession, especially now that the line-out (their weakness) has become so much more valuable than the scrum (their relative strength). To make up for their lack of height and bulk, their rugby motto has been 'quick and clever'.

The influx of bigger men, like Bruce Ferguson of Fiji and the Latus of Tonga, has sadly changed their style of play, and at the Asian Tournament in Kuala Lumpur in October 1994, they began copying the big nations, bashing drably ahead with their forwards. That enabled them to win the tournament and qualify, but it will not take them any further. They are seeded 11th, below the Ivory Coast, but above Italy and Romania, all of which suggests that the seeding method leaves something to be desired.

Their greatest rugby virtues have been their excellent behaviour. They manifest exemplary sportsmanship, with oriental regard for interpersonal relationships, brave commitment, the fitness of men whose main job is rugby, and the illusion of speed as their short, muscular legs flash as they tear about the field.

For the rest of the world, their participation has been important - from a financial point of view. The strength of Japanese rugby has come from the involvement of business - many large companies have teams, resulting in a great number of clubs.

There will not be a better behaved team at the 1995 World Cup than Japan. They will be keen to do what is right and they will be impeccably turned out. Their emblem is the cherry blossom, and for them the cherry on the top is 1995 Rugby World Cup participation.

SQUAD	
Masahiro Kunda - Captain	
Tautomu Matauda	Kazuaki Takahashi
Kiyoshi Imaizumi	Osamu Ota
Lopeti Oto	Kazu Hamabe
Terunori Masuho	Eiji Hirotsu
Yoshihito Yoshida	Bruce Ferguson
Yukio Motoki	Yoshihiko Sakuraba
Tomoyo Haneda	Takashi Akatsuka
Seiji Hirao	Hiroyuki Kajihara
Yoshiji Hirose	Sinali Latu
Katsuhiro Matauo	Ko Izawa
Masami Horikoshi	Sione Latu
Wataru Murata	Akira Yoshida
Masanori Takura	

TEAM MANAGEMENT

Zenzaburo Shirai	Manager
Osamu Koyabu	Coach
Yoshimitsu Konishi	Assistant Coach
Ichiro Kono	Doctor
Akira Minagawa	Physiotherapist

Japanese Rugby Football Union was founded in 1926. Japan's enormous population of 116 million has a growing list of players (currently 52 000 from 1 650 clubs).

Seiji Hirao, Japan's fly half play-maker, sets off on another run.

FRANCE

French rugby is a paradox. It has the greatest depth of outstanding players in the world and yet it makes the weirdest errors in selection. It has the greatest flair and the worst brutality. It provides rugby with glorious romance and base tedium. It is the thinking source of rugby in the world, where genius and madness are too often near aligned. It can reach the pinnacle of glory one day and be plunged into the abyss of crisis the next.

They beat the Springboks and the All Blacks in successive away series and then lost to Scotland in Paris. The paradox of French rugby makes little sense, but it is all the more dangerously unpredictable for that. Nobody can reproduce the magic of a French plan when it comes together.

In 1958 they were the first team ever in sixty-two years to win a series in South Africa, and Lucien Mias wept in incredulous joy. In 1994 they became the fourth team to win a series in New Zealand, and the manner of their achievement was in the best tradition of rugby romance; the best that even France could produce.

It started when Stephen Bachop kicked deep into the French 22 on France's left where captain Phillippe Saint-Andre caught the ball and started running - "because I do not kick so well, you know". The movement crossed the field and swept down the right touch-line with backs and forwards combining. It then careened once more across the field to the left and ended with a try at the New Zealand posts - the winning try in a match that New Zealand, in all conscience, should have won.

French rugby is best when it is filled with calculating passion - the sweeping risky movement where everybody is in control of his body and the direction of play. It is at its worst when individuals allow passion to degenerate into moodiness.

But one thing is absolutely sure: the French have the players and the skills to win the World Cup. They can win or lose to any other team on earth.

SQUAD	
Phillippe Saint Andre - Captain	
Jean-Luc Sadourny	Abdelatif Benazzi
Sebastien Viars	Marc Cecillon
Emile Ntamack	Arnaud Costes
Phillippe Sella	Olivier Merle
Thierry Lacroix	Olivier Brouzet
Franck Mesnel	Olivier Roumat
William Techoueyres	Christian Califano
Christophe Deylaud	Jean-Michel Gonzalez
Yann Delaigue	Laurent Benezech
Guy Accoceberry	Marc de Rougemont
Aubin Hueber	Louis Armary
Laurent Cabannes	Phillippe Gallart
Phillippe Benetton	

TEAM MANAGEMENT	
Guy Laporte	Manager
Pierre Berbizier	Coach
Christophe Mombet	Assistant Coach
Marc Bichon	Doctor
Xavier Gousse	Physiotherapist

Federation Francaise de Rugby was founded in 1920. With 54 million people in total its 218 500 players and 1 782 clubs are in the main in Paris and spread across the south of the country.

A relieving kick for touch on the French line. Another close shave.

TONGA

In the happy South Pacific Islands of sea, sun, hibiscus and perfect waves that make up the Kingdom of Tonga, rugby rules.

The royal dynasty is the oldest in the world. It was well established by the time Captain Cook landed there. The head of that dynasty, King Taufa'ahau Tupou IV who succeeded his mother, Queen Salote, in 1965 after she had reigned for 47 years, gets involved in the game. He goes down to practice and helps the goalkickers, and when his team needed a scrumming machine, he bought them one.

The Friendly Islands, some 180 of them, are not wealthy. At sixteen, each male is given eight and a quarter acres of a land to farm. It is fertile enough to produce enough food to feed its 160 000 population. But money is short. The annual average income is below US$200. For this reason, many people go abroad.

Tongan players, like those of Romania, Argentina, Canada and the Ivory Coast, seek fame and fortune overseas and many have performed well in Japan, the USA, New Zealand and Australia. Their most famous rugby export is the big Wallaby flank, Willy Ofahengaue. Some of its players perform for other countries, but others will return from foreign units, mainly in New Zealand, to join up with the national squad for South Africa.

They got to the World Cup because Western Samoa, whom they beat, were automatic qualifiers after reaching the 1991 World Cup quarter-finals. That left place for another qualifier from the Pacific Rim and Tonga had to beat Fiji to do so. They did so by winning 24-11 at Suva, offsetting their 15-10 defeat at home in the Tongan capital, Nuku'Alofa (Place of Love).

For all their love, friendliness and religious fervour, the rugby players from the islands have a rugged style that has not always endeared them to opponents and has cost them dearly in penalties. Their tackling is brave, but often reckless.

Individual players have exciting flair which, when brought together, creates some of the most vivid and entertaining rugby in the world.

SQUAD

Manakaetau 'Otai - Captain

Takau Lutua	Manu Vunipola
Tu'akalau Fukofuka	Nafe Tufui
'Etuini Talakai	'Elisi Vunipola
Sa'lli Fe'ao	Simana Mafilgo
Fe'ao Vunipola	'Akuila Mafi
Foblisi Masila	Tentan Loto'ahea
Pouvalu Latukefu	Penieli Latu
Falamani Mafi	Alaska Taufa
William Lose	Tevita Va'enuku
Ipolito Fenukitau	Unuoi Va'enuku
Feleti Fakaongo	Safeki Tuipulotu
Feleti Mahoni	Taipe 'Isitolo
Inoke Afeaki	

TEAM MANAGEMENT

Mailefihi Tuku'aho	Manager
Sione Taumoepeau	Coach
Kalauta Kupu	Trainer
Villami Tangi	Doctor

Tonga Rugby Football Union was founded in 1924. Every one of the 160 000 Tongans is touched in some way by rugby. There are 2 457 players in 70 clubs.

The face of Tongan rugby: rugged and determined Tevita Va'enuku on the wing.

IVORY COAST

There has never been a greater surprise in the history of international rugby than the presence of Ivory Coast at the 1995 Rugby World Cup - a greater surprise, even, than if they register a win at the tournament.

The Ivory Coast, like Romania, is the rugby offspring of France. In colonial times many countries plundered the West Coast of Africa. Ivory Coast lost men, firstly to the slave trade and, later, to rugby. France, in particular, benefited from this latter day exile.

In 1973 The Federation Ivoirienne de Rugby was founded. In 1991 the country competed for a place in the Rugby World Cup and brought disgrace on its head when it turned the match with Morocco into such a violent brawl that the referee called a halt to proceedings before full time; the only World Cup game to end prematurely.

In 1991 in Harare, they came last among the qualifiers. In 1994, in Casablanca, they ended first, ahead of Namibia, Zimbabwe, Tunisia and Morocco and so they won a place in the Rugby World Cup of 1995, and everywhere there was astonishment.

Rugby in Ivory Coast, where soccer is the main sport, is confined to the wet coastal area around Abidjan. One family is credited in finding the game a place amongst the Ivoiriennes themselves - Francois Dali and his sons.

Unlike the Romanians, France's other offspring at the World Cup, the Ivoiriennes play their game with abandon. They like the fancy things of rugby life, preferring exhibitionism to hard graft.

They have little by way of international experience. The game in the Ivory Coast has been too poor to allow for international contact outside of the two World Cup tournaments. They do not play even against Senegal, the other Francophone country that produces rugby players. But a South African invitation to its African cousins recently enabled them to have first-hand experience of the highveld, though the resulting defeats at the hands of Northern Transvaal, Western Transvaal and Stellaland could not have sent the elephants home trumpeting in confidence.

SQUAD	
Athanase Dali - Captain	
Ernest Bley	Patrice Pere
Toussaint Djehi	Felix Dago
Jean-Pascal Ezqua	Frederic Dupont
Daniel Quansah	Aboubacar Camara
Achille Niamien	Thierry Kouame
Ble Aka	Lucien Niakou
Gilbert Bado	Aboubacar Soulama
Amidou Kone	Paulin Bouazo
Djakaria Sanoko	Max Brito
Soumaila Kone	Celestin N'Gbala
Ismaila Lassissi	Victor Kouassi
Alfred Okou	Jean Sathicq
Edouard Angoran	

TEAM MANAGEMENT	
Pierre Cassagnet	Manager
Claude-Aime Ezqua	Coach
Dominique Davanier	Assistant Coach
Bile Jean-Louis	Doctor
Mile. Lucie Vabre	Physiotherapist

A relatively new game to this West African nation of 16 million, Federation Ivoirienne de Rugby was established in 1973. Nonetheless, it currently has 2 700 players and 15 clubs.

New boys on the block. The Ivory Coast showed a commendable never-say-die attitude.

SCOTLAND

They sing with great passion "Oh Flower of Scotland" and they play their rugby with serious intent.

For the Scots, cussedness is a national trait. It was ever so. The ancient Romans found them cussed so they built walls to keep the Scots confined to Caledonia, stern and wild. The English found them cussed at Bannockburn when proud Edward's army was sent homeward "tae think again". When they lost to England in 1884, the Scots were cussed again and refused to accept that England's winning try was indeed a try. This dispute led to the formation in 1889 of the International Rugby Board, where, through the years, this cussedness has persisted.

The game in Scotland has always adhered most faithfully to the amateur principle. The Scot who cast this principle in tablets of stone was J. Aikman Smith, who once refused to speak to the King of England because His Majesty had suggested that the Scots wear numbers on their rugby jerseys. "Sire, my players are men, not cattle," Aikman Smith expostulated. They demanded assurance that touring teams adhered to the amateur principle, before allowing them to play north of the Tweed, and they opposed the introduction of the Rugby World Cup because it would endanger their amateur principle.

They are cussed on the field of play, too. The Scots don't give in easily. You may be bigger and faster than they are, but they will tackle and turn the advantage line into a morass in defence of their territory. You may even be better organised than they, and have superior skills in retaining possession, but they will find a way of inserting an endless supply of bodies to frustrate your intent.

The Scottish game is zestful and brave. The country does not have great depth in numbers, confined as the game is to the Border areas and to former pupils of famous schools centred mainly in Edinburgh, yet rugby football has brought Scotland international honour.

For a' that and a' that, they will be rugby men for a' that, and nobody will gainsay their honest endeavour.

Kenny Logan sets off on another of his devastating runs on the wing for Scotland.

S Q U A D	
A G Hastings - Captain	
I C Glasgow	Peter Wright
Craig Joiner	Kevin McKenzie
Kenneth Logan	Kenneth Milne
Anthony Stanger	Stewart Campbell
Scott Hastings	Damian Cronin
Ian Jardine	J F Richardson
Craig Chalmers	Doddie Weir
Andrew Shiel	Iain Morrison
D W Patterson	Ian Smith
Bryan Redpath	Robert Wainwright
Andrew Burnall	Peter Walton
David Hilton	E W Peters
J J Manson	
TEAM MANAGEMENT	
DS Paterson	Manager
DW Morgan	Coach
JR Dixon	Assistant Coach
Mr DAD MacLeod	Doctor
Dr JP Robson	Physiotherapist

Scottish Rugby Union was established two years after England's official body. Scotland's 25 000 players in 276 clubs, playing mainly in the southern half of the country, are drawn from a population of 5 million.

SOUTH AFRICA
THE COUNTRY OF UPLIFTING VISTAS AND SWEEPING CHANGE

Historically, South Africa has been a deeply divided nation. Racial barriers, fuelled by apartheid, and the fears, ignorance and misunderstanding that logically followed, carved canyons between groups and people and eroded the unifying soil of society, washing away the fibre from which to build a future.

This, at least, is what many people may have believed. The opposite was proved when something quite remarkable happened in Cape Town on the 25th May 1995.

The rush hour traffic peaked at 12 noon, and traditional rugby supporters gave fist salutes and sang Shosholoza. Radio Zulu devoted time to explaining the rules of rugby to its listeners and at Newlands Rugby Stadium a jubilant crowd chanted "Nelson, Nelson".

A rainbow display of dancers came together to form a human map of South Africa. And when a man who had spent 27 years in jail as public enemy number one appeared on the field, he got an ovation that would have been fitting for any winning try to be scored during the Rugby World Cup 1995. Who, a few years ago, would have believed us if we had told them that such a thing was possible?

The most magnificent setting of any city in the world. At the foot of Table Mountain, to the right, is the bustling Waterfront and the beaches with sand so white and fine it squeaks like castor sugar under your toes. To the left is Newlands home of South African rugby and the opening of the 1995 Rugby World Cup.

Who would have believed that rugby, that symbol of white male South Africanism, could have such a power to unite and bind our people? And who would have believed that, despite the fact that the South African team is still predominantly an all white team, the entire rainbow nation would rally behind the Boks and cheer for a win?

And yet, out of South Africa's divided past an astonishing reality was forged; a nation that is being re-built on generosity, forgiveness and hope. Out of disunity and racial division, a nation has discovered it's need to put aside bitterness and hatred, a people who are joining hands to bring about change; a people determined to find ways of working things out together.

And although many still carry the burden of wounds from the apartheid era, there is a ground swell of deep commitment to social regeneration, to reconciliation and to redressing the sins of the past.

South Africa is learning from the past and in doing so, may provide a model for others to follow. It is demonstrating that the road to freedom can lead to a common future and that it does not have to go via the torment of civil war.

Since the first democratic elections, South Africa has re-emerged into international dialogue, acceptance and trade, rejoined the Commonwealth and whole-heartedly opened its doors for tourists to discover some of the world's best kept secret destinations.

The human spirit has the power to overcome hatred with love, pain with healing and despair with hope.

The first Rugby World Cup to take place in South Africa symbolised that vision. It celebrated South Africa's welcome back into the international community after long isolation and its acceptance as part of the world family of nations. And, perhaps even more significantly, it paid tribute to the role that sport can play in binding a nation and binding its people. If you train together, play together, and cheer together for one team, you can also work together for the common good. If you engender a spirit of co-operation and goodwill, you light a flame that may burn forever.

It is this flame that South Africa must carry further into every corner of it's diverse society; lighting beacons for the future and guiding people towards lasting and growing national unity. The Rugby World Cup South Africa 1995 has certainly made a significant contribution towards this end.

Although rugby was probably far from the thoughts of President Nelson Mandela in 1990 when he walked to freedom and into the shadow of Table Mountain, it was however fitting to have the opening of the game of the Rugby World Cup in the mother city.

For South Africa as a whole, the occasion holds a special significance. A nation in the process of discovering new ways of behaviour and learning how to accommodate divergent opinions and beliefs was badly in need of a significant experience through which a people could unite in common purpose.

For South Africa, win or lose, the experience of supporting their team performing on the world stage in hard but honest endeavour must strengthen the mortar to hold the bricks of the new democratic edifice together.

This is indeed history being made, as history is being made. The day when all of South Africa united and sang, with tears in its eyes,

God Bless Africa ... Nkosi Sikeleli Afrika.

For South Africa's Minister of Sports and Recreation, Steve Tshwete, Rugby World Cup is a boost to the redevelopment programme for the youth of the country.

THE NINE STADIA

The South African rugby community is privileged. No other country can boast the superb quality of its top class stadia. In a country as large as South Africa it is inevitable that conditions are as varied as the climate and altitude.

Pool 1 and 2 are played at the coast. Pool 3 and Pool 4 have to contend with the more rarefied air of the Transvaal and Free State at altitudes of between one and over one and a half kilometres above sea level. This altitude difference, and its effect on performance, has for years been the topic of intense conversation.

At the coast too, there are differences. Pool 1 shares the milder, wetter winter venues in three cities: stately Newlands, the second oldest test rugby stadium in the world where the smell of tradition permeates the air around the hallowed turf, where there are no spectators, only participants; Boet Erasmus Stadium in Port Elizabeth with its feeling of open space and no nonsense toughness; and the small Danie Craven stadium in Stellenbosch just half an hour's drive east of Cape Town where one game is played in honour of the man who gave a lifetime of service to rugby in South Africa.

Pool 2 played at King's Park in sub-tropical warm, wind-free Durban and Basil Kenyon Stadium in East London. Pool 3 shares its games at the Free State's headquaters in Bloemfontein. and Johanneburg's magnificent Ellis Park, the venue for the final. Pretoria's refurbished Loftus Versveld and Rustenburg's impressive Olympia Park share Pool 4.

But, as Michael Lynagh philosophically points out, the fields are all the same shape and size and the goal posts are all the same width.

Newlands overflowed to break a new attendance record of over 53 000, filling beyond the seating capacity of its newly added grandstand and railway stand. All other host stadia across South Africa completed reconstruction programmes specially for the Rugby World Cup.

It is with great pride and pleasure that I welcome you to the opening of the Rugby World Cup in South Africa.

There can be no greater expression of a nation's pride, nor nobler path to universal understanding than for the cream of its youth to compete on the playing field. It is through their love of the game, their desire to succeed through skill and sacrifice, that mighty links are forged.

In this spirit of healthy rivalry, let play begin. And may the better team win.

NELSON MANDELA   PRESIDENT OF THE REPUBLIC OF SOUTH AFRICA

AUSTRALIA vs SOUTH AFRICA

NEWLANDS • MAY 25 • 15:30

The opening match had all the feeling of a final about it. There was much speculation and tension, reaching a crescendo with the referee's whistle. Before the match Naas Botha said that the team that lost the opening match of the 1995 Rugby World Cup would not win the cup, because the path the loser would have to follow would be too difficult.

He was articulating what most rugby pundits believed. However when the match began, the result seemed irrelevant. South Africa had won before Derek Bevan's whistle was drowned by the roar of the Newlands crowd. The magnificent opening ceremony, stylish yet relaxed, showed all aspects of the rainbow nation's life, as well as welcoming the visitors from other lands in colourful pageantry. It brought proud tears to strong men's eyes, and suddenly the victory over years in the international wilderness made the victory on the field seem less important. South Africa became one team, one nation and it gave its president, Nelson Mandela, an emotional welcome.

Mandela's Springboks played with a passion and disciplined organisation they have not shown since they restarted international competition in 1992. It was a trip back down memory lane to the great days of South African rugby.

They confounded theories that the team that wins the line-outs wins the match, for they tossed line-outs away in the most haphazard fashion; that scrums are just an unimportant way of restarting the match, for they destabilised the Wallaby scrum at crucial times; and that to win the loose ball you need a fast, small man of the David Wilson type, for Wilson was buried with his tight forwards.

The Springboks kicked better and fielded kicks better than the Wallabies. They were prepared for all the fancy stuff in midfield and dumped opponents who increasingly sought the safe haven of their forwards. The Springboks' pressure forced the Wallabies into errors.

Both sides scored two tries each, which may suggest that the match was even closer than the score.

MATCH 1		POOL 1
SOUTH AFRICA	vs	AUSTRALIA
André Joubert	15	Matthew Pini
Pieter Hendriks	14	Damian Smith
Japie Mulder	13	Daniel Herbert
Hennie le Roux	12	Jason Little
James Small	11	David Campese
Joel Stransky	10	Michael Lynagh Ⓒ
Joost vd Westhuizen	9	George Gregan
Rudolph Straeuli	8	Tim Gavin
Ruben Kruger	7	David Wilson
Ⓒ Francois Pienaar	6	Willie Ofahengaue
Hannes Strydom	5	John Eales
Mark Andrews	4	Rod McCall
Ballie Swart	3	Ewan McKenzie
James Dalton	2	Phil Kearns
Pieter du Randt	1	Dan Crowley
REFEREE : Derek Bevan		

Garry Pagel replaced Balie Swart in second half

GAME PROGRESSION
field possesion / time

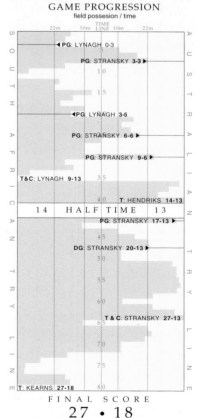

◀ PG: LYNAGH 0-3
PG: STRANSKY 3-3 ▶
◀ PG: LYNAGH 3-6
PG: STRANSKY 6-6 ▶
PG: STRANSKY 9-6 ▶
T&C: LYNAGH 9-13
T: HENDRIKS 14-13
14 HALF TIME 13
PG: STRANSKY 17-13 ▶
DG: STRANSKY 20-13 ▶
T & C: STRANSKY 27-13
T: KEARNS 27-18

FINAL SCORE
27 • 18

MAN OF THE MATCH: JOEL STRANSKY

Tension, pride and all the overwhelming aura of a grand final.
Green and gold meets gold and green on the turf of Newlands.

Rising to the occasion, Stransky darts in for a try which he converted.

The truth is that the Springboks were more superior than the bare statistics indicate and had more scoring chances than the Wallabies. In kinder circumstances they might have scored a handful of tries. If the Wallabies had not been as great and proud a team, the score would have been much higher.

Both sides had heroes. For the Springboks there were plenty - Joel Stransky who outkicked Michael Lynagh, rugby's greatest points machine of all time. Big, cool and fast Andre Joubert at fullback. Pieter Hendriks, with triumphant fist on high, leaving the mighty Campese in his wake. Joost van der Westhuizen was everywhere, varied and committed. Os du Randt and Balie Swart at the scrums, captain Francois Pienaar and Ruben Kruger in tackles, Mark Andrews at kick-off time - the whole lot of them. They were the nation's heroes.

The Wallabies, who started the better side and forced South Africa into mistakes, were heroic, not least in their generosity in defeat, their pride when the going was rough, their skill in the line-outs, their determined defence and the driving play of Willie Ofahengaue. Pressure got to them and they made mistakes they would not normally make, and eventually seemed at their best when they replaced a game plan with a spontaneity which reflected their wonderful skills.

The Australians started the scoring when Michael Lynagh, later to miss two sitters, kicked a penalty goal. Three penalties by Stransky and another by Lynagh put the Springboks ahead 9-6, and then the Wallabies attacked and Lynagh sliced through for a try which he converted (13-9). The South African backs returned the compliment just before the interval with Hendrik's swerving try giving the Boks a half-time lead of 14-13.

The second half, apart from frantic Wallaby attacks at the end belonged to the Springboks. The sweetest moment in the half was Joel Stransky's magical try that sealed the match.

Stransky scored in all four rugby ways - penalty, dropped goal, try and conversion. The man who admitted later he was a nervous wreck before the game, played a match in which he was truly the calm in the storm.

After it was over, people milled around Newlands and in umpteen celebratory groups throughout the city, as if there was no tomorrow. They did not want the day to stop. The whole country was in a state of euphoria. The impossible had been achieved and millions of people bore witness to the sight of one nation, firmly behind one team.

It was the most significant South African event since the election of April 1994.

The danger man, David Campese, was kept in check so as not to release his awsome magic.

"You beauty Mate!"
Australian captain Michael Lynagh crashes down for the first try, which he converted, to nudge Australia into a clear 9 - 12 lead after thirty minutes.

Big Phil Kearns scores Australia's second try.

Hyped up but cool under pressure, Joel Stransky could do no wrong as his drop goal was timed to perfection.

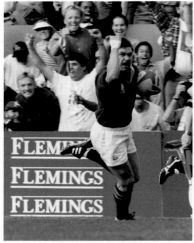

Defiantly Pieter Hendriks punches the air in ecstasy as he crosses the line to give the Springboks a 14-13 lead at half time.

Playing the most important game of his life, Stransky concentrates only on the next few seconds and scores with precision. This was his finest hour.

SCOTLAND vs IVORY COAST

RUSTENBURG • 26 MAY • 16:00

All sorts of records were broken late on a still winter's afternoon in Rustenburg with the sun setting over the hills of the Western Transvaal. How meaningful those records were is uncertain. The Ivoiriennes were simply no match for the Scots, who actually made life harder for themselves than need be by trying to keep the game tight. All they needed to do was spin the ball and run against a team whose players were unfit and unskilled.

When Peter Wright scored his try, Scotland reached 75 points, breaking New Zealand's record of 74 points scored against Italy in the opening match of 1987. By that time Gavin Hastings, the Scottish fullback, had already broken Didier Camberabero's individual record of 30 points, scored against Romania in 1987. Gavin Hastings went on to score 44 points, which was only four points fewer than leading Ivoirienne point scorer, Athanase Dali, had managed in his whole international career. Hastings actually scored all of Scotland's first 27 points, including a hat-trick of tries, the first when he burst through the midfield, collected a wayward bounce that avoided two defenders to touch down at the posts.

Afterwards Hastings said his record did not mean all that much because rugby was a team game. Mind you, he also felt that "we were a wee bit loose".

The Scottish game was not always beyond criticism. Its worst aspect was the behaviour of Peter Wright, whose footwork on the beaten men from the Ivory Coast, deserved far greater censure from Western Samoan referee Felise Vito. But this was a single aberration in an otherwise clinical and impressive performance by the Scots.

The Ivoiriennes scrummed well enough and did better in the line-outs than the Springboks had done against the Wallabies the previous afternoon. They had one really classy player - the scrum-half Frederic Dupont who plays for Nimes in the south of France. He came closest to scoring a try for his team.

It was not a satisfactory match for a World Cup tournament, but necessary for the development of the game in Africa.

Gavin Hastings sets the ball up for another shot at goal on his way to scoring a mammoth 44 points in this game.

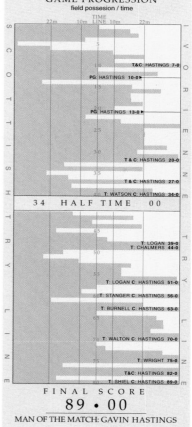

MATCH 2		POOL 4
SCOTLAND	vs	IVORY COAST
© Gavin Hastings	15	Victor Kouassi
Craig Joiner	14	Paulin Bouazo
Tony Stanger	13	Jean Sathicq
Graham Shiel	12	LucienNiakolu
Kenny Logan	11	Celestin N'Gbala
Craig Chalmers	10	Athanase Dali ©
Bryan Redpath	9	Frédéric Dupont
Rob Wainwright	8	Djakaria Sanoko
Ian Smith	7	Ismaila Lassissi
Peter Walton	6	Patrice Pere
Doddie Weir	5	Gilbert Bado
Stewart Campbell	4	Amidou Kone
Peter Wright	3	Toussaint Djehi
Kevin McKenzie	2	Edouard Angoran
Paul Burnell	1	Aka Bley
REFEREE : Felise Vito (Western Samoa)		

Celestin N'Gbala replaced by Max Britto

GAME PROGRESSION
field possesion / time

T&C: HASTINGS 7-0
PG: HASTINGS 10-0 ▶
PG: HASTINGS 13-0 ▶
T & C: HASTINGS 20-0
T & C: HASTINGS 27-0
T: WATSON C: HASTINGS 34-0

34 HALF TIME 00

T: LOGAN 39-0
T: CHALMERS 44-0
T: LOGAN C: HASTINGS 51-0
T: STANGER C: HASTINGS 56-0
T: BURNELL C: HASTINGS 63-0
T: WALTON C: HASTINGS 70-0
T: WRIGHT 75-0
T&C: HASTINGS 82-0
T: SHIEL C: HASTINGS 89-0

FINAL SCORE
89 • 00
MAN OF THE MATCH: GAVIN HASTINGS

Frédéric Dupont, the Ivory Coast scrum half, clears from a wall of solid gold.

FRANCE vs TONGA

ELLIS PARK • 26 MAY • 18:00

It was a tough game for the French, tougher than the score suggests. The Tongans, who started the match with a war dance, were good value, but they made it hard for themselves.

No team can afford to miss six penalty shots at goal, some easy ones, and expect to win. Neither can it afford to take on the French with 14 players, as it did when 22 year old Feleti Mahoni was sent off the field. That was the end of Mahoni's stay in South Africa. It would be a long, lonely journey home to the kingdom of Tonga with the weight of disgrace in his baggage.

Mahoni was sent off for "illegal use of the boot". The victim was Philippe Benetton who was hurt in the incident. It might have been a careless rather than a malicious act and, in any case, it appears that Mahoni might not have been the guilty party.

The disciplinary committee, chaired by Roger Vanderfield, suspended Mahoni for six weeks. It's tough to be from one of the "smaller" unions. Mahoni, who plays his rugby in New Zealand, went home.

When Mahoni was sent off, France was leading 17 - 3, but looked far from convincing. Three-quarters of the second half had elapsed. In those final twelve minutes they scored three tries and made victory look more comfortable and convincing than it was.

The Tongans, whose brand of uncompromising, hard rugby is typical of the Pacific Islands, continued to entertain. No team can take them for granted and even the best dare not relax if they wish to avoid embarrassment.

The Frenchmen, shaved heads and all, played disciplined rugby. They never looked as if they were going to lose, and apart from the splendid passing movement that led to Saint-Andre's try, showed little of their potential.

For France the victory meant that they were safely on their way to the quarter-finals. But coach Pierre Berbizier was not a happy man afterwards. He said that his team was not in the same class as Australia and South Africa. Not too many people took him seriously. Psychologically, being the underdog is often a good position for a rugby team.

MATCH 3   POOL 4

FRANCE vs TONGA

FRANCE		TONGA
Jean-Luc Sadourny	15	Sateki Tu'ipulotu
Emile Ntamack	14	Alasika Taufa
Thierry Lacroix	13	Unuoi Va'enuku
Philippe Sella	12	Penieli Latu
Philippe Saint-Andre	11	Tevita Va'enuku
Jann Delaigue	10	Elisi Vunipola
Aubin Hueber	9	Manu Vunipola
Marc Cecillon	8	Mana Otai
Abdel Benazzi	7	Ipolito Fenukitau
Philippe Benetton	6	Feleti Mahoni
Olivier Brouzet	5	Falamani Mafi
Olivier Merle	4	Willie Lose
Phil Gallart	3	Tu'a Fukofuka
Jean-Michel Gonzalez	2	Fololisi Masila
Lious Armary	1	Sa'ili Fe'ao

REFEREE : Steve Lander (England)

Marc Cecillon replaced by Laurent Cabannes
Falamani Mafi replaced by Inoke Afeaki
Fololisi Masila replaced by Fe'ao Vunipola
Felleti Mahoni sent off

GAME PROGRESSION
field possession / time

DG: DELAIGUE 3-0

PG: LACROIX 6-0

06   HALF TIME   00

PG: LACROIX 9-0

PG: TU' IPULOTU 9-3

PG: LACROIX 12-3

T: LACROIX 17-3

T: HUEBER C: LACROIX 24-3

T: SAINT-ANDRE C: LACROIX 31-3

T&C: LACROIX 38-3

T: VA'ENUKU C: TU' IPHOLTU 38-10

FINAL SCORE
38 • 10

MAN OF THE MATCH: THIERRY LACROIX

A burly Tongan front ranker proves a tough obstacle for the French who only overcame their opponents in the last 20 minutes of the game.

Tongan flanker Mahoni on the tough, lonely walk off the pitch and back to Tonga.

CANADA vs ROMANIA

PORT ELIZABETH • 26 MAY • 20:00

It was expected to be the clash of the minnows which would determine the bottom spot in Pool A - Romania, a team looking to break away from their long standing tradition of 10-man rugby, against the greater discipline, size and athleticism of the men from Canada.

In the end, Canada ran out handsome and impressive winners but, in the eyes of the cognoscenti, this had to be seen in the context of a weaker group not expected to make it to the next round.

The game started evenly with both teams making incursions into the other's territory.

The Romanians set up some attractive backline movements while the Canadians were content to keep it close and pump the touchline.

The first score came after Canada broke out of some sustained Romanian pressure. Captain, Gareth Rees, used his boot to move play downfield with some clever tactical kicks and touchfinders. A move initiated by the forwards led to a try by powerful prop, Rod Snow.

Canada was playing against the wind, but mistakes by the Romanians, turned to advantage by Rees, kept the Canucks on the attack. Four penalties by Rees followed against one by Nicolae Nichitean giving Canada a healthy 17 - 3 lead.

Romania twice failed to find touch and Canada counterattacked, ending in the game's best try for big Al Charron. Colin McKenzie got the last try and Rees, who with this game became the most capped Canadian international by surpassing the 31 caps of Ro Hindson, kept the scoreboard clicking by slotting goals as the men from the Americas enjoyed the benefit of the breeze in the second half.

The Romanians did well in the line-outs, thanks to Constantin Cojocariu and Sandu Ciorascu, but their backs could not turn good ball to their advantage. In the end, Canada turned out to be the more creative team. Fullback, Scott Stewart, coped splendidly with everything that Nichitean lobbed at him. It was his counterattack that led to Charron's try. Canada's loose forwards had a field day. They were brought into play more often as the game progressed and they displayed a subtlety and drive which the Romanians lacked.

Afterwards the Romanian manager, ex-international Theodor Radulescu, faced with the prospect of the Springboks at Newlands for his team's next match, said that he hoped that their effort would be more resolute than it had been against Canada when, he felt, his team had given up.

One felt that it was not a case of giving up, which is uncharacteristic of Romania, but adapting to new and different circumstances.

MATCH 4		POOL 1
CANADA	vs	ROMANIA
Scott Stewart	15	Gheorge Solomie
Winston Stanley	14	Ioan Lucian Colceriu
Christian Stewart	13	Nicolae Raleanu
Steve Gray	12	Romeo Gontineac
Doug Lougheed	11	Ionel Rotaru
© Gareth Rees	10	Nicolae Nichitean
John Graf	9	Daniel Neaga
Colin McKenzie	8	Ovidiu Slusariuc
Ian Gordon	7	Adrian Gealapu
Al Charron	6	Traian Oroian
Mike James	5	Constantin Cojocariu
Glenn Ennis	4	Sandu Ciorascu ©
Rod Snow	3	Gabriel Vlad
Mark Cardinal	2	Ionel Negreci
Eddie Eans	1	Gheorghe Leonte
REFEREE : C. Hawke (New Zealand)		

Nicolae Nichitean replaced by Ilie Ivanciuc
Daniel Neaga replaced by Vasile Flutur

GAME PROGRESSION
field possesion / time

T: SNOW 5-0
PG: REES 8-0
PG: NICHITEAN 8-3
PG: REES 11-3

11 HALF TIME 03

PG: REES 14-3
DG: REES 17-3
T: CHARRON C: REES 24-3
PG: REES 27-3
T: McKENZIE C: REES 34-3

FINAL SCORE
34 • 03

MAN OF THE MATCH: GARETH REES

Canada's John Graf meets solid resistance from a resolute Romanian defence..

One Canadian attack that does not get through

WEST SAMOA vs ITALY

EAST LONDON • 27 MAY • 13:00

If the Western Samoans were the surprise package of the 1991 tournament, the side touted as most likely to usurp their status as giant-killers in 1995 was Italy. The only problem was that someone had forgotten to tell the Samoans.

Gone was the memory of the seventy point hiding at the hands of the Wallaby world champs, the same team that the Italians had come within an ace of turning into world chumps on their tour of Australia.

The hallmark of the Pacific islanders' spectacular performance in 1991 was to the fore once again as they overwhelmed the Italians at Basil Kenyon Stadium. A potent amalgam of pride, pace and sheer physical presence proved too much for Italy. The torpedo-like tackling, strong-running and quality support play which had so unhinged Wales four years earlier, again looked capable of winning the Samoans a quarter-final berth.

Nowhere was this more evident than in the play of their bristling centre pairing of To'o Vaega and Tupo Faamasino. When this dynamic duo weren't punching holes in the Italian midfield they were rattling their bones with ferocious tackling.

The Italian backs were literally knocked out of their stride and Samoa's two first-half tries, scored by wingers Brian Lima and George Harder, were a direct consequence of midfield incursions which created overlaps.

The other crucial factor was the Italian pack's inability to live up to its billing as a competent, ball-winning unit. They failed to put the suspect Samoan scrummage to the test and were similarly unable to take control at the line-out, an area in which the islander's are notoriously vulnerable.

The Samoans revelled in the abundant possession, running the ball from deep. Italy was fortunate to be only a point adrift at half-time (12 - 11) when a late try by Marcello Cuttitta supplemented a penalty and drop-goal by fly-half Diego Dominguez.

Having got the measure of their opponents, the Samoans were in no mood to throttle back and further tries followed for Lima, number 8 Shem Tatupu, and two intercept tries in the last two minutes from fly-half Darren Kellett and Harder. Paulo Vaccari got one back for Italy, but it could hardly have been called compensation for their shattered dreams.

MATCH 5		POOL 2
WEST SAMOA	vs	ITALY
Mike Umaniga	15	Paola Vaccari
Brian Lima	14	Massimo Ravazzolo
To'o Vaega	13	Ivan Fracescato
Tupo Faamasino	12	Massimo Bonomi
George Harder	11	Macello Cuttitta
Darren Kellett	10	Diego Dominguez
Tu Nuualiitia	9	Alessandro Troncon
Shem Tatupu	8	Carlo Checcinato
Junior Paramore	7	Julian Gardner
Sila Vaifale	6	Orazio Arancio
Darryl Williams	5	Pierpaolo Pedroni
Lio Falaniko	4	Roberto Favaro
© Peter Fatialofa	3	Franco Properzi
Tala Leisamaivao	2	Carlo Orlandi
Mike Mika	1	Massimo Cuttitta ©
REFEREE : J Dume		

Lio Falaniko replaced by Tata Leiasamaivao

GAME PROGRESSION
field possession / time

```
                 TIME
        22m   10m LINE 10m   22m
S
A    ◄ DG: DOMINGUEZ  0-3
M                              10           T: LIMA C: KELLETT 7-3
O    ◄ PG: DOMINGUEZ  7-6
A                              15           T: HARDER 12-6
                               20
N                              25
                               30
                               35
T: CUTTITTA 12-11              40
     1 2   HALF TIME   1 1
T                              45
R                                           T: LIMA 17-11
Y                              50
                                            T: TATUPU C: KELLETT 24-11
                               55
                               60
L    PG: KELLETT 27-11 ►
I    T: VACCARI C: DOMINGUEZ 27-11
N                              70
E                                           PG: KELLETT 30-18 ►
                               80           T&C: KELLETT 37-18
                                            T: HARDER 42-18
```

FINAL SCORE
42 • 18
MAN OF THE MATCH: BRIAN LIMA

The West Samoan forwards with a rare line-out ball against Italy.

Despite the attention of two defenders, West Samoan George Harder scores a try in his side's opening match against Italy .

WALES
vs JAPAN

BLOEMFONTEIN • 27 MAY • 15:00

The magnificent new Free State Stadium played host in its first major event to a truly international occasion; teams from Japan and Wales, referee from Argentina and touch judges from Ireland and Italy. Playing for Wales was a New Zealand Maori, and in the Japanese side were four players from the South Pacific islands. It all happened in Bloemfontein. The Japanese won the hearts of the Free State crowd, not only because they showed bravery against their bigger, more experienced opponents, but also because of their adventurous, exciting style of play. Japanese rugby may be lacking in brute force, but it is never boring.

When it became obvious that full-back, Tsutomu Matsuda, was not going to succeed with even the simplest kicks at goal, the Japanese decided to run everything. What a thrill to see a team launching an attack from a set piece on its own goal line in order to get out of trouble, and make a fine attacking play from a deeply-thrown lineout ball. Both Japan's tries, scored by Lopeti Oto, were out of the top drawer.

Attractive, yes. Entertaining, without a doubt. But in the real world of modern international rugby, they were no match for the efficient driving play of the Welsh and the accurate boot of Neil Jenkins, at centre for this game.

Wales, playing in unfamiliar green strip, were never in danger of losing. They, too, scored wonderful tries, the quality of which helped raise the general tenor of the game as a spectacle.

Gareth Thomas had a dream debut, scoring three tries. Ieuan Evans, the former captain, improved his Welsh record to 23 tries when he collected a kick ahead for a well-taken score. Their Maori flanker, Hemi Taylor, too, had a very effective match.

Injuries to lock, Derwyn Jones, the tallest man at the tournament, and fly-half Adrian Davies, who twisted an ankle, created concern in the Welsh camp. David Evans, who replaced Davies, was the first cap from Treorchy in decades. Another concern for Wales may have been their level of fitness, although their fade may have been due more to easing up when they had a comfortable lead, than lack of puff on the highveld. All in all, it was a happy day in Bloemfontein.

MATCH 6		POOL 4
WALES	vs	JAPAN
Tony Clement	15	Tsutomu Matsuda
Ieuan Evans	14	Lopeti Oto
© Mike Hall	13	Akira Yoshida
Neil Jenkins	12	Yukio Motoki
Gareth Thomas	11	Terunori Masuho
Adrian Davies	10	Seiji Hirao
Andy Moore	9	Masami Horikoshi
Emyr Lewis	8	Sione Latu
Hemi Taylor	7	Sinali Latu
Stuart Davies	6	Hiroyuki Kajihara
Gareth Llewellyn	5	Bruce Ferguson
Derwyn Jones	4	Yoshihiko Sakraba
John Davies	3	Kuzuaki Takahashi
Garin Jenkins	2	Masahiro Kunda ©
Mike Griffiths	1	Osamu Ota
REFEREE : Efraim Sklar (Argentina)		

Adrian Davies replaced by David Evans
Derwin Jones replaced by Stuart Roy

GAME PROGRESSION
field possesion / time

	TIME	
22m	10m LINE 10m	22m

PG: JENKINS 3-0 ►

PG: JENKINS 6-0 ►

15

20

PG: JENKINS 9-0 ►

25

T: MOORE C: JENKINS 16-0

T: EVANS C: JENKINS 23-0

30

35

PG: JENKINS 26-0 ►

T: EVANS 31-0   T: THOMAS 36-0

36   HALF TIME   00

45

T: THOMAS C: JENKINS 43-0

50

55

60

T: OTO 43-5

65

70

75

T: THOMAS C: JENKINS 50-5

T: TALOR C: JENKINS 57-5

80

T: OTO 57-10

FINAL SCORE
57 • 10

MAN OF THE MATCH: GARETH THOMAS

Welsh number 8, Emyr Lewis has time to one hand the ball to his back line

Banzai! The Japanese on the charge. Whilst ultimately outgunned by Wales, they won admiration for their adventurous play.

ENGLAND vs ARGENTINA

DURBAN • 27 MAY • 17:00

There was nothing tongue in cheek about Will Carling's post-match reflections. In fact he seemed to have difficulty in finding the right words to describe how England, one of the pre-tournament favourites, had managed to avoid an earth-shattering defeat. All he could manage was, "To win when you play that badly is ... something."

Something indeed. And most of that something was embodied in the right boot of fly-half Rob Andrew who rescued them from defeat with yet another impeccable kicking display, scoring all England's points by way of six penalties and two drop-goals.

The Argentinians, who had the satisfaction not only of scoring the only two tries of the game but also leaving England reeling on the ropes during the second half, played with enormous commitment and a game plan clearly focused on their strength in the tight five and, ultimately, were unlucky to come second.

Although the English had the better of the early "feeling out" exchanges and built a comfortable 12 - 0 half-time lead thanks to the Argentine failure to observe the off-side law in the loose (duly punished by Andrew), there were clear signs that the wheels might fall off the English wagon.

The Pumas' main weapon, their scrummage, was wounding English confidence. Spearheaded by a front-row of Matias Corral, Federico Mendez and Patricio Noriega, arguably the best in the world, they denied England the stable platform essential to their attacking patterns, particularly those involving the back-row giants Ben Clarke and Tim Rodber.

The Pumas were not slow to seize the initiative as their confidence grew in the second half. Lisandro Arbizu got Argentina off the mark with a penalty but they fell behind when a drop-goal and penalty from Andrew took England to 18 - 3. The Pumas displayed the greater drive and continuity in the loose with flanker Rolando Martin outstanding.

The Pumas reaped their reward when the burly Noriega muscled over from a flying wedge penalty. Argentina, despite a huge Andrew drop-goal and late penalty, dominated the final quarter with Arbizu bringing richly deserved respectability to the scoreline with a penalty and a last-minute try, leaving England with plenty to ponder.

MATCH 7 — POOL 2

ENGLAND vs ARGENTINA

England		Argentina
Mike Catt	15	Ezequiel Jurado
Tony Underwood	14	Diego Albanese
Jeremy Guscott	13	Diego Cuesta Silva
© Will Carling	12	Sebastian Salvat ©
Rory Underwood	11	Martin Teran
Rob Andrew	10	Lisandro Arbizu
Dewi Morris	9	Rodrigo Crexell
Steve Ojomoh	8	Jose Maria Santamarina
Ben Clarke	7	Cristian Viel
Tim Rodber	6	Rolando Martin
Martin Bayfield	5	German Llanes
Martin Johnson	4	Pedro Sporleder
Victor Ubogu	3	Patricio Noriega
Brian Moore	2	Frederico Mendez
Jason Leonard	1	Matias Corral

REFEREE : J. M. Fleming (Scotland)

GAME PROGRESSION
field possession / time

TIME

PG: ANDREW 3-0

PG: ANDREW 6-0

PG: ANDREW 9-0

PG: ANDREW 12-0

12 HALF TIME 00

DG: ANDREW 15-0
PG: ARBIZU 15-3
PG: ANDREW 18-3
T: NORIEGA C: ARBIZU 18-10
DG: ANDREW 21-10
PG: ARBIZU 21-13
T: ARBIZU 24-18
PG: ANDREW 24-13

FINAL SCORE
24 • 18

MAN OF THE MATCH: ROB ANDREW

Argentina's front ranker, Patricio Noriega is driven over the England try line by his pack, in an adaptation of their famous bajada scrum, to score their first try.

England's fly-half Rob Andrew, in a burst of acceleration, shows he can run as well as kick.

NEW ZEALAND vs IRELAND

JOHANNESBURG • 27 MAY • 20:00

Jonah Lomu, the giant 20-year-old New Zealand wing, burst onto the rugby firmament like a new sun rising on an world hungering for an icon to illuminate the rugby union game. He came to Ellis Park with his All Black colleagues to take on the fiery Irish at their uncompromising best. And, although the All Blacks revealed a wealth of impressive talent on the day, no other individual made the impact that Lomu made, to such devastating effect.

The Irish started proceedings by singing their new rugby anthem, "Ireland's Call", and began the match at a frantic pace. Typically swarming, shoving, throwing bodies into the fray, hacking ahead and launching slick counterattacks, they led 7 - 6 (a converted try to two penalties) until Lomu took a hand. Sweeping down the left wing with the irresistible momentum of a steam engine, he had tacklers bouncing every which way off his powerful frame.

Two tries in quick succession by Lomu and Bunce for the All Blacks were countered by one from Dennis McBride for Ireland. Had Eric Elwood had his kicking boots on, Ireland might have kept themselves in the game. Andrew Mehrtens, on the other hand, was deadly accurate and was instrumental in giving New Zealand a handy lead at half-time.

After the re-start, Lomu got his second try and New Zealand seemed to have the game sewn up. Lomu underlined the threat he poses as the All Blacks started a move in their own 22. The big wing swept down-field, bumping off tacklers like so many pesky insects. Simon Geoghegan, covering from the left wing, eventually got his arms around Lomu's ankle and managed to hang on - but it was too late. A quick transfer of the ball to Josh Kronfeld ranging up on the inside led to the dynamic young flanker diving over for the try.

The crowd, squarely in underdog Ireland's corner at the start, cheered in admiration for this very efficient All Black performance. Initially the New Zealanders had been placed below Australia, England and South Africa in the rankings. But after this match it was obvious that if any team was going to win the World Cup in 1995, this All Black team was the one to beat.

MATCH 8		POOL 1
NEW ZEALAND	vs	IRELAND
Glen Osborne	15	Jim Staples
Jeff Wilson	14	Richard Wallace
Frank Bunce	13	Brendan Mullin
Walter Little	12	Jonathan Bell
Jonah Lomu	11	Simon Geoghegan
Andrew Mehrtens	10	Eric Elwood
Graham Bachop	9	Michael Bradley
Michael Brewer	8	Paddy Johns
Josh Kronfeld	7	Dennis McBride
Jamie Joseph	6	David Corkery
Blair Larsen	5	Neil Francis
Ian Jones	4	Gabriel Fulcher
Olo Brown	3	Garret Halpin
© Sean Fitzpatrick	2	Terry Kingston ©
Craig Dowd	1	Nick Popplewell

REFEREE : Wayne Erickson (Australia)

Jeff Wilson replaced by Marc Ellis
Michael Brewer replaced by Kevin Schuler
Sean Fitzpatrick temporarily. replaced by Norm Hewitt
Jim Staples replaced by Maurice Field
Jonathan Bell temporarily replaced by Maurice Field

GAME PROGRESSION
field possesion / time

T: HALPIN C: ELWOOD 0-7
PG: MEHRTENS 3-7
PG: MEHRTENS 6-7
T: LOMU C: MEHRTENS 13-7
T: BUNCE C: MEHRTENS 20-7
T: McBRIDE 20-12

20 HALF TIME 12

T: LOMU 25-12
PG: MEHRTENS 28-12
T: KRONFELD 33-12
PG: MEHRTENS 36-12
T: CORKARY C: ELWOOD 36-19
T: OSBORN C: MEHRTENS 43-19

FINAL SCORE
43 • 19

MAN OF THE MATCH: JONAH LOMU

Irish fullback Jim Staples and All Black wing Jeff Wilson collide in mid-air. Staples ended up with a broken hand and was out of the World Cup and Wilson took no further part in the game.

Try scorer Frank Bunce quickly checks his options as a blaze of Irish green threatens.

WEST SAMOA
vs ARGENTINA

EAST LONDON • 30 MAY • 12:30

rgentina may have come second in this pulsating contest and subsequently bowed out of the tournament, but they will be remembered as the side that proved that the scrummage is far from being an obsolete weapon in the modern game.

In a match that was a superb contrast of two styles, the all-running-handling Western Samoans against the grinding strength of the "gauchos", the Islanders' sheer athleticism, flair and courage won the day, but they took a terrible mauling from the Pumas in the process. Three of the Samoan heroes, flanker Junior Paramore, with a fractured wrist, and no.6 Shem Tatupu, with torn shoulder muscles, paid the price for their sterling defence, while fly-half Darren Kellett was ruled out of the tournament with a dislocated shoulder.

The pounding from the mighty Pumas scrum started in the sixth minute when, passing up the chance of three points for a penalty, the Argentines opted for a 5 metre scrum. They pulverised the Samoan scrummage into conceding a penalty try as they collapsed in disarray on their own line leaving referee Dave Bishop no choice.

The Samoans struck back immediately when, showing their willingness to run the ball from anywhere on the field, Kellett and Vaega put flying winger George Harder away to level the score.

With the Argentine pack rumbling ominously upfield through prodigious rolling mauls and the Samoans replying with glorious but sporadic counterattacks, the goal-kickers were soon pressed into service. The Pumas, learning from the error of going into the England game without a kicker, were well served by young flyhalf, Jose Cilley, whose three penalties to Kellett's one gave Argentina a 16-10 half-time lead. After the break the Pumas scored another pushover try from a 5 metre scrum through scrum-half Rodrigo Crexell and, with Kellett and Cilley exchanging further penalties, led 26-13 going into the final quarter.

The Samoans responded by producing one of rugby's great comebacks. They were kick-started by Kellett who capitalised on the Pumas lack of composure under fire with three more penalties, narrowing the gap to 26-22 with seven minutes remaining. Then, sparked by superb runs from Paramore, a remarkable two-try burst from Laupepe and Lam in the last five minutes clinched the match, but not before they yet again had to put themselves on the line to stop a last, desperate Pumas assault in the closing seconds.

MATCH 4		POOL 1
ARGENTINA	vs	WEST SAMOA
Ezequiel Jurado	15	Mike Umaga
Diego Cuesta Silva	14	Brian Lima
Lisandro Arbizu	13	To'o Vaega
© Sebastian Salvat	12	Tupo Fa'amasino
Martin Teran	11	George Harder
Jose Cilley	10	Darren Kellett
Rodrigo Crexell	9	Tu Nu'ualiitia
Jose Santamarina	8	Pat Lam ©
Cristian Veil	7	Junior Paramore
Rolando Martin	6	Shem Tatupu
Pedro Sporleder	5	Potu Leavasa
German Llanes	4	Lio Falaniko
Patricio Noriega	3	George Latu
Frederico Mendez	2	Tala Leasamaivao
Matias Corral	1	Mike Mika
REFEREE : D. Bishop (New Zealand)		

George Harder replaced by George Laupepe

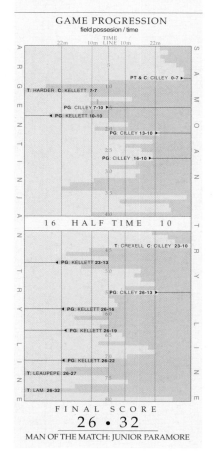

GAME PROGRESSION
field possesion / time

PT & C: CILLEY 0-7
T: HARDER C: KELLETT 7-7
PG: CILLEY 7-10
PG: KELLETT 10-10
PG: CILLEY 13-10
PG: CILLEY 16-10

16 HALF TIME 10

T: CREXELL C: CILLEY 23-10
PG: KELLETT 23-13
PG: CILLEY 26-13
PG: KELLETT 26-16
PG: KELLETT 26-19
PG: KELLETT 26-22
T: LEAUPEPE 26-27
T: LAM 26-32

FINAL SCORE
26 • 32

MAN OF THE MATCH: JUNIOR PARAMORE

The hard, physical game of the Western Samoans contributed greatly to their win over Argentina, and advanced them into the quarter finals.

Western Samoan fly-half Darren Kellett scored 17 points in the bruising match.

SOUTH AFRICA vs ROMANIA

NEWLANDS • 31 MAY • 14:30

I am not sure what was supposed to come after the Lord Mayor's show, but if it was a donkey cart it would fit the Springbok performance in the wake of the splendour of their World Cup opening-match victory over the Wallabies. They won this time, which they were required to do, but the manner of the victory was slow, ponderous and at times asinine.

The Newlands crowd once again showed its opening-match euphoria, but it was soon deflated and by half-time the crowd was fed up. For want of something better to do they did Mexican waves, banged a drum and screeched on a bugle.

Not 10 minutes into the game and the Springboks disintegrated into a loose, planless group of individuals, trying, it seems, to make some point to the selectors. They must have had a game plan, but apparently they abandoned it. Adriaan Richter had captained with great distinction the mid-week team of dirt trackers on the Australian tour. However, this side had no distinction. The dream castle built on Ascension Day Thursday had crumbled.

In the crowd there was a banner that read: *Forget Sex Appeal ... Get Boks Appeal.* Sex appeal may well have been the more appealing.

Not that the Boks did not want to please. When last did you see a Springbok team run two penalties slap in front of the opposition's posts? They seemed to forget about the basics - short passes on a windy day, passing in front of the man, backing up, getting into position, varying play, getting to the loose ball first, playing as a team.

Romania were proud, purposeful and determined. They got to break-downs first, in numbers and cohesively. They won line-outs, but sadly, they kicked far too much. At the end, their stockily built centres, who with ease blotted out Brendan Venter and Christiaan Scholtz, ran and showed great potential.

Romania's try came from a sharp break by Nicolae Raceanu and speedy support from Andrei Guranescu. It may not have been one of the most memorable tries of the World Cup but it brought the eastern Europeans much joy and was far more spectacular than the Springboks' mastodon flop-overs.

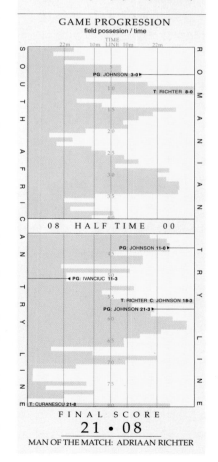

MATCH 10		POOL 1
SOUTH AFRICA	vs	ROMANIA
Gavin Johnson	15	Vasili Brici
James Small	14	Lucian Colderiu
Christiaan Scholtz	13	Nicolae Raceanu
Brendan Venter	12	Romeo Gontineac
Pieter Hendricks	11	Ghoerge Solomie
Hennie Le Roux	10	Ilie Ivanciuc
Johan Roux	9	Vasile Flutur
ⒸAdriaan Richter	8	Tiberiu Brinza Ⓒ
Robbie Brink	7	Alexandru Gealapu
Ruben Kruger	6	Andrei Guranescu
Krynauw Otto	5	Constantin Cojocariu
Kobus Wiese	4	Sandu Ciorascu
Marius Hurter	3	Gabriel Vlad
Chris Rossouw	2	Ionel Negreci
Garry Pagel	1	Gheorge Leonte
REFEREE : Ken McCartney (Scotland)		

Brendan Venter temporarily replaced by Joel Stransky

GAME PROGRESSION
field possesion / time

PG: JOHNSON 3-0 ►

T: RICHTER 8-0 ►

08   HALF TIME   00

PG: JOHNSON 11-0 ►

◄ PG: IVANCIUC 11-3

T: RICHTER C: JOHNSON 18-3 ►

PG: JOHNSON 21-3 ►

T: CURANESCU 21-8

FINAL SCORE
21 • 08
MAN OF THE MATCH: ADRIAAN RICHTER

Vasile Flutur spins and dive passes the ball away to his fly-half at Newlands, on the day the Romanians will proudly remember

New cap Robbie Brink turns for support from his captain Adriaan Richter as Vasile Brici tackles.

FRANCE vs IVORY COAST

RUSTENBURG • 30 MAY • 18:00

It was just a penalty goal, not a winning penalty goal, and yet the ecstasy on the faces of the Ivoiriennes suggested that it was a miracle. They had scored their first points in the World Cup tournament, and against their mentors and heroes, France, where nine members of the team play their rugby. You could have sworn they were the winning points in a victorious game. But then, for the men from West Africa, there was a great deal riding on scoring points - a little normal pride, for example.

Ivory Coast, in their first outing, had helped Scotland and Gavin Hastings into the record books. This time the Ivoiriennes were far more resolute in their play. They got little ball from the big, skilled French pack but they tackled with far more purpose and, in the end, ecstasy became transport to heaven as they scored two tries.

The French, to their credit, played the game in all ways. They were disciplined, self-controlled and patient, even when their physical superiority dominated. They ran and ran all over the show, mostly as individuals, at times selfishly, but adventurously and at speed. The game had an element of fun and the underdogs did well enough to please the crowd. The most exciting of the French was captain Phillippe Saint-Andre.

Some of the tries were splendid, none more so than that scored by Sebastian Viars, though none was as dramatic as that by Aboubacar Camara after charging down a kick. The last score of the match provided a generous ending - an Ivory Coast intercept, a kick ahead, a hack on and eventually the try by Aboubakar Soulama.

The star of the match, for the men from Cote d'Ivoire, was Frederic Dupont, the scrum half who plays for Nimes in France. He was here, there and everywhere. His decisions were accurate and his speed of service excellent, despite playing behind a fairly ragged pack of forwards.

There was an interesting communication in the match when the Korean referee, Moon Soo Han, who has no English, gave an Ivoirienne a talking-to - or rather a gesturing-to.

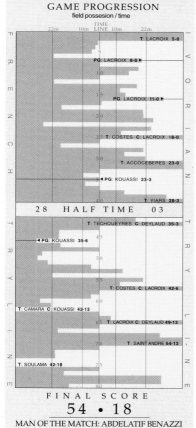

MATCH 11		POOL 4
FRANCE	vs	IVORY COAST
Sebastian Viars	15	Victor Kouassi
William Techoueyres	14	Aboubakar Soulama
Thierry Lacroix	13	Jean Saticq ©
Franck Mesnel	12	Lucien Niakou
©Philippe Saint-Andre	11	Max Brito
Yann Delaigue	10	Aboubacar Camara
Guy Accoceberry	9	Frederic Dupont
Arnaud Costes	8	Ismalia Lassisi
Abdelatif Benazzi	7	Alfred Okou
Laurent Cabannes	6	Patrice Pere
Olivier Brouzet	5	Djakaria Sanoko
Olivier Roumat	4	Gilbert Bado
Christian Califano	3	Toussaint Djehi
Marc de Rougemont	2	Achille Niamien
Laurent Benezech	1	Jean-Pascal Ezoua

REFEREE : Moon Soo Han (Korea)

Yann Delaigue replaced by Christophe Deylaud.
Djakaria Sanoko replaced by Amidou Kone
Toussaint Djehi replaced by Ernest Bley
Jean-Pascal Ezousa temp. replaced by Ernest Bley

GAME PROGRESSION
field possesion / time

T: LACROIX 5-0
PG: LACROIX 8-0
PG: LACROIX 11-0
T: COSTES C: LACROIX 18-0
T: ACCOCEBERES 23-0
PG: KOUASSI 23-3
T: VIARS 28-3

28 HALF TIME 03

T: TECHOUEYRES C: DEYLAUD 35-3
PG: KOUASSI 35-6
T: COSTES C: LACROIX 42-6
T: CAMARA C: KOUASSI 42-13
T: LACROIX C: DEYLAUD 49-13
T: SAINT ANDRE 54-13
T: SOULAMA 42-18

FINAL SCORE
54 • 18

MAN OF THE MATCH: ABDELATIF BENAZZI

French full back Sebastian Viars caught in possession

Burly French lock Oliver Roumat leaps free from a despairing Ivoirienne tackle

SCOTLAND vs TONGA

PRETORIA • 30 MAY • 20:00

Gavin Hastings broke another record. This time he kicked eight penalty goals, a record for the World Cup, and he equalled the number of penalty goals scored in any test match. He kicked extremely well. The men from the Friendly Islands gave him the chance to kick well.

This was the worst-tempered match of the first two rounds of the 1995 World Cup. It did not quite erupt into warfare but it went beyond niggle.

The Tongans were still aggrieved at the sending off and despatch home of their man Felati Mahoni in their previous match, and they were feeling generally hard-done-by. They had less respect for the laws of the game, its official minister and their opponents than was good for the game.

The scoring tells its own story. Hastings kicked his eight penalties before Scotland had even scored a try, by which time the score was 24 - 5. Tonga, running with verve and directness, had scored the first try. It was their first chance to run with the ball and flanker Ipolito Fenukitau latched onto a popped-up ball and plunged over for an excellent try.

Scotland forwards dominated the game. Tonga were desperate, and therefore not clever, in their efforts to counter the bigger Scots. The forwards made the try for no. 8 Eric Peters. Gavin Hastings's try in the corner, after a finely judged pass from his brother Scott, was the Scotland highlight of a largely unpleasant evening. At the death Scott Hastings was credited with a try, after which the Tongans vented their verbal wrath on the referee.

In their opening match of the tournament the big men had hammered it out, without any aggressive or dirty play, for a full game - and then in this match, which nobody could have enjoyed, tempers became frayed. Not that all the blame could be laid at the Tongans' door. The crowd's sympathies, vociferous and undignified as it was, were largely with the Tongans. And the Scots did not always contain their emotions the way the French had done.

Gavin Hastings deserves to do well. His is the wholesome face of international rugby.

MATCH 12		POOL 4
SCOTLAND	vs	TONGA
© Gavin Hastings	15	Sateki Tu'ipulotu
Craig Joiner	14	Alasika Taufa
Scott Hastings	13	Unuoi Va'enuku
Ian Jardine	12	Penieli Latu
Kenneth Logan	11	Tevita Va'enuku
Craig Chalmers	10	Elisi Vunipola
Derrick Patterson	9	Manu Vunipola
Eric Peters	8	Mana Otai ©
Robert Wainwright	7	Ipolito Fenukitau
Iain Morrison	6	Inoke Afeaki
Damian Cronin	5	Pouvalu Latukefu
Doddy Weir	4	William Lose
Peter Wright	3	Tu'akalu Fukofuka
Kenny Milne	2	Fe'ao Vunipola
David Hilton	1	Sa'illi Fe'ao
REFEREE : Barry Leask (Australia)		

Peter Wright replaced by Paul Burnell
Maun Vunipola replaced by Nafe Tufui

GAME PROGRESSION
field possesion / time

PG: HASTINGS 3-0 ▶
PG: HASTINGS 6-0 ▶
PG: HASTINGS 9-0 ▶
T: FUNOKITAU 9-5
PG: HASTINGS 12-5 ▶
PG: HASTINGS 15-5 ▶
PG: HASTINGS 18-5 ▶

18   HALF TIME   05

PG: HASTINGS 21-5 ▶
PG: HASTINGS 24-5 ▶
T: PETERS 29-5
T: HASTINGS 34-5
T: S.HASTINGS C: G.HASTINGS 41-5

FINAL SCORE
41 • 05

MAN OF THE MATCH: DODDY WEIR

Tongan scrumhalf Manu Vunipola, one of three brothers in the team, tries to clear under Scottish pressure as faces in the pack are etched in serious intent.

Gavin Hastings turns away satisfied as one of his eight penalty goals heads for the posts.

AUSTRALIA
vs CANADA

They lost on 25 May and all the world wondered. They won on 31 May and still the world wondered. Were the Australians pulling some sort of con trick or were they just battling to find their magic touch?

For a while on this Wednesday afternoon they looked the Wallabies of old, dominant at forward and skilful behind, and they led 17 - 0 while the Canadians looked on, apparently bemused. There was a moment of vintage Wallaby play as Jason Little cut through, drew the defence and set the powerful new boy Joe Roff speeding over for a try.

Then things started to change. Captain Gareth Rees, who proved that there was far more to his play than just a precise boot, kicked a penalty. And then Mark Hartill put his foot on an opponent's face, an act that in a previous game had seen a Tongan sent home. Hartill was allowed to continue without even a warning. Later Phil Kearns was warned twice, once for a punch and once for stomping. Both Hartill and Kearns later left the field injured. Even David Campese showed petulance when tackled. Perhaps the Wallabies were too uptight, for this was not the usual face of Australian rugby. Whether tension was the cause is not known, but the Wallabies did not run away with Canada as they had threatened to do. More and more Canada took the game to the Wallabies, doing many of the Wallabies' best things better than the Wallabies themselves.

Australia moved to a 27 - 6 lead, but Canada did not stop trying and some of the most thrilling passages of World Cup play followed, as Canada drove close and wide to be followed immediately by Wallaby counterattack. Canada showed a level of skill not usually associated with their game. Al Charron eventually got over for a try after Canada had hurled assault after assault at the Wallaby line.

The lively second half ended after each side had scored a try.

Both sides lost important players. Three Wallabies, Kearns, Hartill and Peter Slattery, and big Gareth Rowlands for Canada, left the field before the end of play.

MATCH 13		POOL 1
AUSTRALIA	vs	CANADA
Mathew Burke	15	Scott Stewart
Joe Roff	14	Winston Stanley
Tim Horan	13	Christian Stewart
Jason Little	12	Steve Gray
David Campese	11	David Lougheed
© Michael Lynagh	10	Gareth Rees ©
Peter Slattery	9	John Graf
Tim Gavin	8	John Hutchinson
Ilie Tabua	7	Al Charron
Willie Ofahengaue	6	Gordon MacKinnon
John Eales	5	Mike James
Warwick Waugh	4	Gareth Rowlands
Mark Hartill	3	Rod Snow
Phil Kearns	2	Karl Svoboda
Tony Daly	1	Eddie Evans

REFEREE : Patrick Robin (France)

Gareth Rowlands replaced by Glenn Ennis
Peter Slattery replaced by George Gregan
Mark Hartill replaced by Euen McKenzie
Phil Kearns replaced by Mike Foley

GAME PROGRESSION
field possesion / time

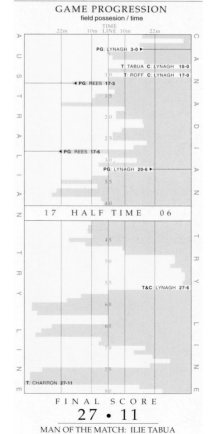

FINAL SCORE
27 • 11
MAN OF THE MATCH: ILIE TABUA

Canada's Winston Stanley comes to the solid defensive block of Michael Lynagh and Peter Slattery in the Port Elizabeth thriller.

Despite a 17-6 deficit against them, Canada mounted a sterling effort in the second half.

IRELAND vs JAPAN

"Ja-pan, Ja-pan, Ja-pan", chanted the Free Staters in Bloemfontein's new stadium. They loved the eager, adventurous men from Japan, who deserved better than defeat by 22 points.

The crowd "booed" the South African referee when he penalised their special guests, who had made Bloemfontein their headquarters for the World Cup. One Japanese supporter from the Free State waved an old South African flag in one hand and a Chinese flag in the other - which may have made sense to him.

The match was another of those classics - broadsword versus rapier, with the broadsword of pounding forwards beating the rapier thrust of quick-silver backs, but it was only apparent on the scoreboard. For one thing, Japan hardly ever kicked - their only kicks at goal were conversions - choosing rather to run from impossible positions and they ran for their rugby.

Ireland's tries were at close quarters, except for Simon Geoghegan's. Japan's tries came from long movements. The most spectacular were those of Ko Izawa from a tapped penalty and veteran Seiji Hirao's from a run-around.

There were smaller contests as well - Japanese inventiveness against Irish power in these line-outs; the battle of the two lively scrum halves, little Niall Hogan who at 1.72m towered over even livelier Masa Horikoshi's 1.58m; and there were six skilful, energetic loose forwards on the field - all of which helped to keep the game going.

This was a historic occasion for South Africa. Stef Neethling was the first South African referee to take charge of a World Cup match. And he added to history by awarding two penalty tries to Japan as they wilted before the Irish scrummaging on their goal line.

So, in the city of flowers, the three leaves of Ireland's shamrock defeated the three cherry blossoms of Japan. But it was a good day for rugby football and a credit to the World Cup.

MATCH 14		POOL 3
IRELAND	vs	JAPAN
Conor O'Shea	15	Tsu Matsuda
Richard Wallace	14	Lopeti Oto
Brendan Mullin	13	Akira Yoshida
Maurice Field	12	Yukio Motoki
Simon Geoghegan	11	Yositikuru Yoshida
Paul Burke	10	Seiji Hirao
Niall Hogan	9	Masa Horikoshi
Paddy Johns	8	Sione Latu
Eddie Halvey	7	Sinali Latu
David Corkery	6	Hiro Kajihara
Neil Francis	5	Bruce Ferguson
David Tweed	4	Yoshihada Sakuraba
Paul Wallace	3	Masanori Takura
Keith Wood	2	Masahro Kunda Ⓒ
Ⓒ Nick Popplewell	1	Osamu Ota

REFEREE: S. Neethling (South Africa)

Eddie Halvey temp. replaced by Anthony Foley
David Tweed replaced by Anthony Foley
Keith Wood replaced by Terry Kingston
Sinali Latu replaced by Ko Izawa

GAME PROGRESSION
field possesion / time

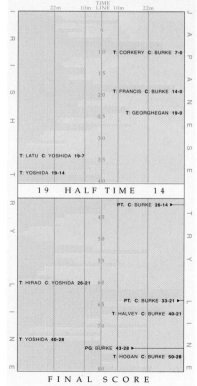

	TIME		
T: CORKERY C: BURKE 7-0			
T: FRANCIS C: BURKE 14-0			
T: GEORGHEGAN 19-0			
T: LATU C: YOSHIDA 19-7			
T: YOSHIDA 19-14			

19 HALF TIME 14

| PT. C: BURKE 26-14 ▶ |
| T: HIRAO C: YOSHIDA 26-21 |
| PT. C: BURKE 33-21 ▶ |
| T: HALVEY C: BURKE 40-21 |
| T: YOSHIDA 40-28 |
| PG: BURKE 43-28 ▶ |
| T: HOGAN C: BURKE 50-28 |

FINAL SCORE
50 • 28

MAN OF THE MATCH: SINALI LATU

ENGLAND vs ITALY

DURBAN • 31 MAY • 17:00

I n rain-drenched conditions at King's Park, England failed to live up to their billing as one of the pre-tournament favourites.

Italy took the game to England from the kickoff but came unstuck when Tim Rodber claimed loose ball on his own 22 to spark a lethal counterattack. The ball was whipped wide by Phil de Glanville and Mike Catt to release Tony Underwood to scorch home from 40 metres out.

Stand-in captain Rob Andrew converted and then added a penalty to punish an offside by Italy to give England a 10 - 0 lead. Italy fly-half Diego Dominguez got his side off the mark with a penalty midway through the half, but the reconstituted England pack - with Rowntree at loosehead, Leonard switched to tighthead and Back brought in at openside - mounted enough pressure to give Andrew two more kicks at goal.

However, England, with the linchpin of their pack no. 8 Dean Richards still sidelined due to hamstring trouble, were unable to impose themselves upfront against a lively Italy pack spearheaded by the two Italo-Australians flanker Julian Gardner and lock Mark Giacheri. A minute from half-time, a Catt clearance was charged down by winger Paolo Vaccari who followed up to score. Dominguez's conversion narrowed the gap to 16 - 10.

After the interval England again got off to a flying start when, following a Bayfield line-out "take" and a series of forward drives, a cut-out pass from Andrew saw Catt put Rory Underwood over in the corner. England at last seemed to have got Italy's measure, and when two further penalties from Andrew gave them a 27 - 10 cushion, they seemed to be content to coast to the quarter-final.

The Azzurri had other ideas. They punished England's lack of rigour to dominate the last 15 minutes of the match, forcing Catt to make a try-saving recovering tackle on Francescato, and then scoring a deserved last-minute try when captain Massimo Cuttitta barged his way over, with Dominguez converting.

MATCH 15		POOL 2
ENGLAND	vs	ITALY
Mike Catt	15	Luigi Troiani
Tony Underwood	14	Paolo Vaccari
Phil De Glanville	13	Ivan Francescato
Jeremy Guscott	12	Stefano Borden
Rory Underwood	11	Mario Gerosa
© Rob Andrew	10	Diego Dominguez
Kyran Bracken	9	Alessandro Troncon
Ben Clarke	8	Julian Gardner
Neil Back	7	Orazio Arancio
Tim Rodber	6	Andrea Sgorlon
Martin Bayfield	5	Mark Giacheri
Martin Johnson	4	Pierpaulo Pedroni
Jason Leonard	3	Franco Properzi
Brian Moore	2	Carlo Orlandi
Graham Rowntree	1	Massimo Cuttitta ©
REFEREE : S. Hilditch (Ireland)		

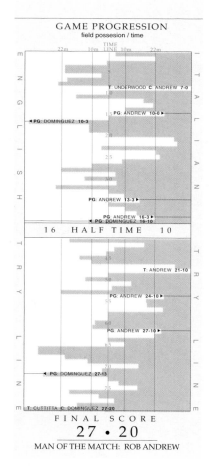

GAME PROGRESSION
field possesion / time

T. UNDERWOOD C. ANDREW 7-0
PG. ANDREW 10-0 ►
◄ PG: DOMINGUEZ 10-3
PG: ANDREW 13-3 ►
PG. ANDREW 16-3 ►
◄ PG: DOMINGUEZ 16-10

16   HALF TIME   10

T. ANDREW 21-10 ►
PG. ANDREW 24-10 ►
PG. ANDREW 27-10 ►
◄ PG: DOMINGUEZ 27-13
T. CUTTITTA C. DOMINGUEZ 27-20

FINAL SCORE
27 • 20

MAN OF THE MATCH: ROB ANDREW

England's downfield kick stops in safe Italian hands inside the touchline.

Tony Underwood and Mike Catt find their way blocked by the resolute Italians at King's Park in Duban.

NEW ZEALAND vs WALES

It is a mark of New Zealand's impressive performance at this stage of Rugby World Cup 1995 that many pundits thought Wales, despite their 34 - 9 drubbing, did well in their outing against the All Black juggernaut. The men from the Valleys were well organised and played with fire and discipline but were no match for the better equipped Kiwis.

With awesome efficiency and concentration, fierce in Jamie Joseph, clinical in Andrew Mehrtens and uncompromising in Josh Kronfeld, New Zealand went about as effective a demolition job as could be witnessed anywhere.

Jonah Lomu's influence on the game was underlined by the attention he received from the number of Welshmen who descended on him every time the ball made its way to his wing. Despite the attempt to smother him, he managed to get away for a telling 60 metre charge late in the game that led to Kronfeld's try. At this level a team needs just one of these in the game to win a test. Andrew Mehrtens once more proved that he is a worthy successor to Grant Fox. Not only did he kick at goal with precision but when he hoofed the ball down-field, it travelled a prodigious distance, and his snapped pass to Walter Little, which led to a try at the posts, spoke of artistic skill. Throughout the match the All Blacks were poised to take advantage of any mistakes, and there were a number, and turn them into points.

For Wales, the halfbacks were magnificent, especially Robert Jones who stood up bravely to enormous pressure. Neil Jenkins was the picture of concentration and kicked well. The Welsh line-outs were well organised, and at the start, and again at the end of the match, the forwards drove well. But, in the final balance, it was not enough against a team that appears to have no chinks in its armour.

Wales has not beaten New Zealand in 42 years; they will have to wait a little longer on the evidence that this still young New Zealand team is about to launch a new era of great All Black rugby. Nowhere is the difference more marked than the two teams' attitude towards the result. The Welsh used to sing about a 9 - 3 margin; the All Blacks were silent about 34 - 9. Just a job, mate

MATCH 16		POOL 3
NEW ZEALAND	vs	WALES
Glen Osborne	15	Tony Clement
Jonah Lomu	14	Iuean Evans
Walter Little	13	Mike Hall ©
Frank Bunce	12	Gareth Thomas
Marc Ellis	11	Wayne Proctor
Andrew Mehrtens	10	Neil Jenkins
Graeme Bachop	9	Robert Jones
Michael Brewer	8	Hemi Taylor
Josh Kronfeld	7	Mark Bennett
Jamie Joseph	6	Gareth Llewellyn
Blair Larsen	5	Greg Prosser
Ian Jones	4	Derwyn Jones
Olo Brown	3	John Davies
© Sean Fitzpatrick	2	Jonathan Humphreys
Craig Dowd	1	Ricky Evans
REFEREE : Ed Morrison (England)		

Eric Rush replaced Jonah Lomu

GAME PROGRESSION
field possesion / time

DG: JENKINS 0-3
PG: MEHRTENS 3-3
T: LITTLE C: MEHRTENS 10-3
PG: MEHRTENS 13-3
T: ELLIS C: MEHRTENS 20-3
DG: JENKINS 20-6
20   HALF TIME   06
PG: MEHRTENS 23-6
PG: MEHRTENS 26-6
DG: JENKINS 26-9
PG: MEHRTENS 29-9
T: KRONFELD 34-9

FINAL SCORE
34 • 09

MAN OF THE MATCH: ANDREW MEHRTENS

Robert Jones of Wales eludes Marc Ellis of New Zealand when the two teams met at Ellis Park. Both had outstanding matches.

Derwyn Jones may be taller but his feet are on the ground as All Black lock, Blair Larsen, gets up high to win line-out ball.

TONGA vs IVORY COAST

RUSTENBURG • 3 JUNE • 13:00

The match started with tragedy. The 3 June 1995 was a black day for rugby and the Rugby World Cup. Max Brito, the Ivory Coast wing, collected a high ball in the opening minutes of the game and tried to run out of trouble. A fairly innocuous tackle resulted in a ruck and when it broke up Brito was on his back, paralysed. A helicopter was called in to ferry him to hospital in Pretoria. It was the worst moment in the eight years of the World Cup competition.

It was a niggling, ill-tempered match and the two teams did their negative best to ensure that they did not end up bottom of their pool in the competition. The better equipped Tongans had too much savvy for their naive opponents whose main struggle was with even the basic laws of the game.

That said, the Ivoiriennes were enormously popular in Rustenburg where the locals gave them their full and vociferous support. The team showed its appreciation after the final whistle by trotting round Olympia Park waving to their hosts in appreciation.

The West Africans' play improved greatly after the shambles of their first match. They brought with them the dying art of the grubber kick, which was their main ploy to break the defensive line. Their own defence, too, became more resolute in this game, especially after Djakaria Sanoko came onto the field. He is a classy forward, having played in winning French selections against the Springboks and the All Blacks.

The Tongans understood the game better. They were able to organise their play, move the ball wide and change the direction of attack very effectively. Their game is totally uncompromising and their treatment of their fellow man when he is a rugby opponent belies the fact that they are a deeply religious people.

Tonga never looked likely to lose the match and led 24 - 0 before Ivory Coast put the first score on the board via a penalty kick by Athanase Dali. Another try to each side and a penalty by Dali made up the scoring. The final whistle was somewhat of a relief - it was not an affable exposition of rugby football.

Without their less familiar red (Tongan) and gold (Ivoirienne) jerseys, both teams looked less conspicuous playing in white with trim.

MATCH 17   POOL 4

TONGA	vs	IVORY COAST
Safeki Tuipulotu	15	Victor Kouassi
Penieli Latu	14	Aboubacar Soulama
Simana Mafilgo	13	Jean Sathicq Ⓒ
Unuoi Va'enuku	12	Lucien Niakou
Tevita Va'enuku	11	Max Brito
'Elisi Vunipola	10	Aboubacar Camara
Nafe Tufui	9	Frederic Dupont
Ⓒ Manakaetau 'Otai	8	Ismaila Lassissi
William Lose	7	Alfred Okou
Inoke Afeaki	6	Patrice Pere
Falamani Mafi	5	Soumaila Kone
Pouvalu Latukefu	4	Gilbert Bado
'Etuini Talakai	3	Toussaint Djehi
Fe'ao Vunipola	2	Edouard Angoran
Tu'akalau Fukofuka	1	Ernest Bley

REFEREE : Don Reordan (U.S.A.)

Unuoi Va'enuku replaced by Taipe 'Isitolo
Tu'akalau Fukofuka replaced by Takau Latua
Max Brito replaced by Thierry Kouame
Aboubacar Camara replaced by Athanase Dali
Patrice Pere replaced by Djakaria Sanoko

GAME PROGRESSION
field possesion / time

PG: TUIPULOTU 3-0

PT: C: TUIPULOTU 10-0

T: LATUKEFU C: TUIPULOTU 17-0

T: OTAI C: TUIPULOTU 24-0

24   HALF TIME   00

PG: DALI 24-3

PG: DALI 24-6

T: TUIPULOTU 29-6

T: OKOU 29-11

FINAL SCORE
29 • 11

MAN OF THE MATCH: MANAKAETU 'OTAI

Moments later, Max Brito (number 11) was taken from the field paralysed.

AUSTRALIA vs ROMANIA

STELLENBOSCH • 3 JUNE • 15:00

The first international match ever played at the picturesque university town of Stellenbosch, as a gesture of respect to the memory of Dr Danie Craven, was graced by world champions Australia and Romania - a country the good doctor always wanted to have make a rugby pilgrimage to South Africa.

The Wallabies, whose gold jerseys were too close to the Romanians' deep yellow, turned out in their alternative strip of green and gold hoops. They also fielded their alternative players against what turned out to be the weakest team in their pool.

But Romania certainly were no slouches. They had given the Springboks a tough game during the week and Australia had been displaying less than full confidence in their previous showings. It did not help the Wallabies' jittery start when Ilie Ivanciuc gave his team a 3 - 0 lead with a well-taken dropped goal from in front of the posts.

Australia started asserting their greater skills through their forwards with the impressive Ilie Tabua in the vanguard of a series of charges. At half-time they led 14 - 3, thanks to tries by Mike Foley and one of the "finds" of the tournament, winger Joe Roff.

In the second half the Australians seemed to regain their old confidence, and with it, their ball playing skills. Romania on the other hand, instead of exploiting the overlap, wasted hard-won possession by booting the ball downfield into the hands of the wingers who had dropped back in defence.

The single most impressive individual of the latter part of the game was the towering lock John Eales. Apart from his general play and the example he set for his less experienced team mates, his accurate and prodigious kicks for goal enabled him to convert all four second-half tries. But it was far from being a one-man show. Scott Bowen, in his first international since 1993, the back row of Tim Gavin, David Wilson and Ilie Tabua, and stand-in captain Rod McCall all contributed to an improved performance.

The Romanians can take heart from some good quality rugby despite going down in all three matches in what proved to be the most evenly balanced of the pools.

MATCH 18		POOL 1
AUSTRALIA	vs	ROMANIA
Matthew Burke	15	Vasile Brici
Damian Smith	14	Lucien Colceriu
Daniel Herbert	13	Nicolae Recean
Tim Horan	12	Romeo Gotineac
Joe Roff	11	Gheorge Salomie
Scott Bowen	10	Ilie Ivanciuc
George Gregan	9	Vasile Flutur
Tim Gavin	8	Tiberiu Brinza ©
David Wilson	7	Alexandru Gealapu
Ilie Tabua	6	Andrei Guranescu
John Eales	5	Constantin Cojocariu
© Rod McCall	4	Sandu Ciorascu
Ewen McKenzie	3	Gabriel Vlad
Michael Foley	2	Ionel Negreci
Tony Daly	1	Gheorge Leonte

REFEREE : Naoki Saito (Japan)

George Gregan replaced by Peter Slattery
David Wilson temporarily replaced by Daniel Manu
Romeo Gotineac replaced by Adrian Lungu
Ionel Negreci replaced by Valere Tufa

GAME PROGRESSION
field possesion / time

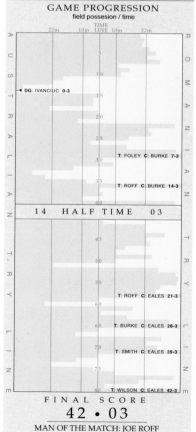

DG: IVANCIUC 0-3

T: FOLEY C: BURKE 7-3

T: ROFF C: BURKE 14-3

14 HALF TIME 03

T: ROFF C: EALES 21-3

T: BURKE C: EALES 28-3

T: SMITH C: EALES 35-3

T: WILSON C: EALES 42-3

FINAL SCORE
42 • 03

MAN OF THE MATCH: JOE ROFF

Despite solid confrontations by the Romanian defenders, Foley and Roff broke through for tries in the first half.

One down, two to go. Wallaby Matthew Burke bounds through the open space and scores.

FRANCE vs SCOTLAND

PRETORIA • 3 JUNE • 17:00

Emile Ntamack, the elusive, hard to stop French wing, scored in the last movement of the game after almost five minutes of injury time to give France a sensational victory over Scotland in a match billed as the eliminator - the loser being set up for a confrontation with the All Blacks in the knockout rounds of the tournament.

Trailing 19 - 15, and the referee indicating that there was one minute left to play, France launched a series of attacks deep into the Scottish 22. A quickly won loose scrum saw the ball move swiftly along the backs with Scotland in desperate defence against the French charge. Ntamack appeared from the right wing, took the pass, showed the ball to his man outside and crashed through two Scottish tackles to score far out, giving his side a one-point lead when time expired.

Thierry Lacroix added the extra two points to keep intact his 100% record of five penalties and a conversion. In essence, this turned out to be the difference between the two sides. The usually reliable boot of Gavin Hastings let him down while Lacroix could not put a foot wrong.

This was a match that Scotland should have won. It was reminiscent of the match in Paris earlier this year when the boot was on the other foot and Gavin Hastings came bursting down the middle of the field for a try and victory.

The game lived up to its promise of being a hammer and tongs affair and the Scots started with great fire and commitment. They were not headed until the final French effort. Rob Wainwright scored the first try when Gavin Hastings counterattacked from 40 metres out after Jean-Luc Sadourny failed to find touch. When Hastings converted from the corner, Scotland led 13 - 3.

The intensity of the exchanges caused a number of long stoppages for injury, the most serious of which were broken arms for French no. 8 Phillippe Benetton and scrum-half Guy Accoceberry.

With Lacroix keeping the French in touch with his accurate kicking, the stage was set for the last dramatic movement, which snatched victory from the jaws of defeat.

MATCH 19   POOL 4

SCOTLAND vs FRANCE

© Gavin Hastings	15	Jean-Luc Sadourny
Craig Joiner	14	Emile Ntamack
Scott Hastings	13	Phillippe Sella
Andrew Shiel	12	Thierry Lacroix
Kenny Logan	11	Phillippe Saint Andre ©
Craig Chalmers	10	Christophe Deylaud
Bryan Redpath	9	Guy Accoceberry
Eric Peters	8	Phillippe Benetton
Iain Morrison	7	Laurent Cabannes
Rob Wainwright	6	Abdelatif Benazzi
Doddie Weir	5	Olivier Roumat
Damian Cronin	4	Olivier Merle
Peter Wright	3	Christian Califano
Kenny Milne	2	Jean-Michel Gonzalez
David Hilton	1	Laurent Benezech

REFEREE : Wayne Erickson (Australia)

Andrew Shiel replaced by Ian Jardine
Peter Wright replaced by Andrew Burnall
Phillippe Benetton replaced by Marc Cecillon
Guy Accoceberry replaced by Aubin Hueber

GAME PROGRESSION
field possession / time

PG: HASTINGS 3-0 ►
◄ PG: LACROIX 3-3
PG: HASTINGS 6-3 ►
T: WAINWRIGHT C: HASTINGS 13-3

13   HALF TIME   03

◄ PG: LACROIX 13-6
◄ PG: LACROIX 13-9
PG: HASTINGS 16-9 ►
◄ PG: LACROIX 16-12
PG: HASTINGS 19-12 ►
◄ PG: LACROIX 19-15
T: N'TAMACK C: LACROIX 19-22

FINAL SCORE
19 • 22

MAN OF THE MATCH: EMILE NTAMACK

Led by Gavin Hastings, it was Scotland, Scotland all the way ... until the last, nail-biting, thrilling few seconds of the game.

The face of two captains. Victory at the whistle for Phillippe Saint Andre as Gavin Hastings's thoughts turn 'All Black'.

SOUTH AFRICA
vs CANADA

PORT ELIZABETH • 3 JUNE • 20:00

It is being called the Battle of Boet Erasmus. The Ascension Day euphoria of the opening match at Newlands descended into disgrace at Port Elizabeth. A portent of things going horribly wrong on the night was the failure of the stadium lights just after the singing of the two national anthems.

The brawl that broke out with 10 minutes of the game to run was easily one of the most unsavoury incidents to occur in rugby at international level. The disciplinary committee took firm and justifiable action and it earned five players, Pieter Hendriks and James Dalton of South Africa - who were banned from any further part in the competition - and Canadians Rod Snow, Gareth Rees and Scott Stewart, long suspensions.

From the start the Boks took a stranglehold on proceedings. The South African scrum was impressive and their line-out forwards seemed to have sorted out their problems. Two push-over tries awarded to Adriaan Richter, both converted by Joel Stransky, and two penalties by Stransky saw the local team take a 20 - 0 lead, after having led 17 - 0 at half-time.

Then the fired-up Canadians came back. For the rest of the game the Springboks threw everything into cast-iron defence that was more than equal to the onslaught. The sheer physical aspect of this stage of play may have been the catalyst that gave rise to the petulant bout of shoving between Hendriks and Winston Stanley that led to the uncalled-for intervention of Stewart and the free-for-all that followed.

When peace was restored, the referee, after consulting with his experienced touch judge, sent Dalton, Snow and Rees off the field. A subsequent viewing of the match video resulted in the citing of Hendriks and Stewart and their suspension for 90 days and 60 days respectively.

It was a night filled with tension and drama that ended in ignominy. A final word: the Rugby World Cup officials deserved praise for their consistency and determination in censuring outbreaks of violence that bring a noble game into disrepute.

MATCH 20		POOL 1
SOUTH AFRICA	vs	CANADA
Andre Joubert	15	Scott Stewart
Gavin Johnson	14	Winston Stanley
Brendan Venter	13	Christian Stewart
Christiaan Scholtz	12	Steve Gray
Pieter Hendriks	11	David Lougheed
Joel Stransky	10	Gareth Rees ©
Johan Roux	9	John Graf
Adriaan Richter	8	Colin McKenzie
Robby Brink	7	Gordon MacKinnon
© Francois Pienaar	6	Ian Gordon
Hannes Strydom	5	Al Charron
Kobus Wiese	4	Glenn Ennis
Marius Hurter	3	Rod Snow
James Dalton	2	Mark Cardinal
Garry Pagel	1	Eddie Evans
REFEREE : Dave McHugh (Ireland)		

Gavin Johnson replaced by Joost van der Westhuizen
Hannes Strydom replaced by Krynauw Otto
Joel Stransky replaced by Hennie le Roux
Colin McKenzie replaced by Chris Michaluk
Glenn Ennis replaced by John Hutchinson

GAME PROGRESSION
field possesion / time

PG: STRANSKY 3-0 ▶

T: RICHTER C: STRANSKY 10-0

T: RICHTER C: STRANSKY 17-0

17   HALF TIME   00

PG: STRANSKY 20-0 ▶

FINAL SCORE
20 • 00

MAN OF THE MATCH: ADRIAAN RICHTER

Christian Stewart and a blaze of Maple Leaves close in on Christiaan Scholtz. Springbok captain Francois Pienaar creates a movement for the loose ball.

After the all-in brawl, captain Gareth Rees and Rod Snow along with Springbok James Dalton are sent off.

ARGENTINA vs ITALY

EAST LONDON • 4 JUNE • 13:00

The rugby links between these Latin cousins have not always been all sweetness and light, particularly given the exodus of leading Argentine players to the Italian game over the past decade. Consequently there was plenty to play for, not least pride.

The Italians fired the more impressive final salvo in a sparkling encounter thanks to Diego Dominguez, their Argentine born-and-bred fly-half. Dominguez stole away for the winning try on the stroke of time after an opportunist interception, which he then converted.

In a seven-try thriller this last-gasp effort was the difference between victory and defeat for Italy, who trailed 25 - 24 at the time, and was the icing on the cake of a Dominguez performance that reaped him 21 points. His four first-half penalties kept Italy in the hunt, with the sides locked at 12 - 12 at the interval, after the powerful Argentine pack had dominated the early exchanges.

Initially the Pumas looked as if they might overwhelm the Azzurri upfront. They trumped an early try by tireless flanker Rolando Martin by bludgeoning their way to a penalty try five minutes before the break courtesy of their fearsome *bajada* scrummage, fly-half Jose Cilley converting.

In the second half the Italian pack, with captain Massimo Cuttitta to the fore, scavenged enough ball off the Pumas to give their talented backline a chance to show their flair. They were duly rewarded with spectacular tries by wingers Paolo Vaccari - Dominguez converting - and Mario Gerosa, to give Italy a commanding lead going into the final quarter.

The Pumas were stung into action and struck back with tries from powerhouse prop Martin Corral and then, with only eight minutes remaining, Cilley. That gave them a one-point lead, but it would have been more substantial had the young Puma fly-half managed more than a penalty and a conversion from his seven kicks at goal during the match.

Where Argentina failed to make the most of their chances, the same could not be said of Italy - specially the irrepressible Dominguez.

Despite solid Azzuri tackling by Ivan Francescato (12) and Andrea Sgorlon (7), the Argentinian Pumas kept the ball alive in a very evenly contested match.

Azzurri scrumhalf Alessandro Troncon covers his opposite number Rodrigo Crexell.

NEW ZEALAND
vs JAPAN

BLOEMFONTEIN • 4 JUNE • 15:00

I t was the type of game that everyone present was pleased to witness but sad to recall. In years to come the spectators will relate that they were there when the record books were so comprehensively rewritten, but nobody, least of all New Zealand, can take much pleasure in the fact that the vanquished was the adventurous, entertaining team from Japan.

One hopes that the Japanese rugby authorities do not see this enormous defeat as a loss of face; nobody else does. It was unfortunate that a side so deficient in height and physical strength came up against one of the finest teams in world rugby at their irrepressible best. The spirit of the men from the Land of the Rising Sun was well illustrated by the two tries they scored, both by Hiroyuki Kajihara. This was in itself a feat - there are not many players who can claim to have scored two tries in a match against the All Blacks.

The All Blacks ran, handled and backed up superbly. They roamed all over the field in search of space and they simply did not let up. Crucially, the Japanese forwards simply could not compete on anything like equal terms in the battle for possession.

The All Blacks broke just about every record in the book: 145 points is the most scored by a team in the World Cup tournament, beating the 89 by Scotland against the Ivory Coast; 21 tries is the most scored by a team in the World Cup tournament, beating the previous best of 13, which Scotland equalled against the Ivory Coast; 45 points, by Simon Culhane, is the highest individual total in a match in the World Cup tournament, passing the 44 scored by Gavin Hastings against the Ivory Coast; 45 points is the highest by a player in Test debut, beating the 29 by Andrew Mehrtens against Canada; 20 conversions by Simon Culhane is the most by an individual or a team in a Test; and 6 tries by Marc Ellis is the greatest number by one individual in any Test match.

The All Blacks advance to the quarter-finals while the Japanese go back to the drawing board.

MATCH 22		POOL 3
NEW ZEALAND	vs	JAPAN
Glen Osborne	15	Tautomu Matauda
Eric Rush	14	Lopeti Oto
Marc Ellis	13	Akira Yoshida
Alama Ieremia	12	Yukio Motoki
Jeff Wilson	11	Yoshihito Yoshida
Simon Culhane	10	Yoshiji Hirose
Ant Strachan	9	Wataru Murata
Zinzan Brooke	8	Sinali Latu
© Paul Henderson	7	Ko Izawa
Kevin Schuler	6	Hiroyuki Kajihara
Blair Larson	5	Bruce Ferguson
Robin Brooke	4	Yoshihiko Sakuraba
Richard Loe	3	Kazuaki Takahashi
Norm Hewitt	2	Masahiro Kunda ©
Craig Dowd	1	Osamu Ota

REFEREE : George Gadjovich (Canada)

Blair Larson replaced by Jamie Joseph
Sinali Latu replaced by Takashi Akatsuka

GAME PROGRESSION
field possesion / time

		TIME			
	22m	10m	LINE	10m	22m

T. RUSH C. CULHANE 7-0
T. LOE C. CULHANE 14-0
T. ELLIS C. CULHANE 21-0
T. ELLIS C. CULHANE 28-0
T. R.BROOKE C. CULHANE 35-0
T. OSBORNE C. CULHANE 42-0
T. IEREMIA C. CULHANE 49-0
T. CULHANE C. CULHANE 56-0
T. WILSON C. CULHANE 63-0
T. ELLIS C. CULHANE 70-0
◄ PG. HIROSE 70-3
T. WILSON C. CULHANE 77-3
T. RUSH C. CULHANE 84-3

84   HALF TIME   03

T. OSBORNE 89-3
T. ELLIS C. CULHANE 96-3
T. KAJIHARA C. HIROSE 96-10
T. DOWD C. CULHANE 103-10
T. R.BROOKE C. CULHANE 110-10
T. KAJIHARA C. HIROSE 110-17
T. ELLIS C. CULHANE 117-17
T. ELLIS C. CULHANE 124-17
T. RUSH C. CULHANE 131-17
T. WILSON C. CULHANE 138-17
T. HENDERSON C. CULHANE 145-17

FINAL SCORE
145 • 17
MAN OF THE MATCH: MARC ELLIS

There were many heroes for the Kiwi supporters including Marc Ellis whose tornado twisting path left his Japanese opponents unable to stop his record-making six tries.

Culhane also had his share of records with 45 points in this match.

IRELAND
vs WALES

While this sudden-death playoff ultimately failed to live up to its billing, there were enough thrills and spills, Celtic passion, courage and spontaneity to make up for the technical deficiencies of both sides.

In the end it was the Irish who raised their arms in triumph as they progressed to the quarter-finals for the third World Cup in succession. For the Welsh there was the bitterness of defeat - out of the quarter-finals for the second World Cup in a row. There would be dark questions asked in the valleys, not least about an uninspired forward effort.

The Irish started proceedings exactly as expected - total onslaught fuelled by fierce passion. In as many minutes they led 14 - 0 with two well-taken tries - the first when Nick Popplewell wrenched his way over, and the other after Denis McBride peeled off the back of the line-out 40 metres out and, despite being brought to ground, was not held, regained his feet and streaked away from the cover to touch down under the posts. Eric Elwood converted both tries.

Neil Jenkins kept the Welsh in the game with three penalty goals and his team looked set to improve its 9 - 14 deficit when replacement flanker Eddie Halvey rounded off an Irish attack with a determined assault on the try line. Elwood's conversion gave the Irish a 21 - 9 cushion.

But the men in red did not throw in the towel. A try by Jonathan Humphreys, converted by Jenkins, brought the score to a more attainable target of 21 - 16. The Welsh were now putting everything into the attack against their tiring opponents. The red tide struck again and again at the advantage line and the Irish were hard pressed to repel them. Then a penalty to Ireland on one of the few occasions play moved into the Welsh half resulted in an Elwood goal (24 - 16) that was to prove to be the winning kick.

For the Welsh an injury-time try by Hemi Taylor came too late. The final whistle blew seconds later and Ireland had squeezed home 24 - 23 to earn a place in the knockout stages.

MATCH 23		POOL 3
IRELAND	vs	**WALES**
Conor O'Shea	15	Anthony Clement
Richard Wallace	14	Ieuan Evans
Brendan Mullin	13	Mike Hall ©
Jonathan Bell	12	Neil Jenkins
Simon Geoghegan	11	Gareth Thomas
Eric Elwood	10	Adrian Davies
Niall Hogan	9	Robert Jones
Paddy Johns	8	Emyr Lewis
Denis McBride	7	Hemi Taylor
David Corkery	6	Stuart Davies
Neil Francis	5	Gareth Llewellyn
Gabriel Fulcher	4	Derwyn Jones
Gary Halpin	3	John Davies
© Terry Kingston	2	Jonathan Humphreys
Nick Popplewell	1	Mike Griffiths
REFEREE : Ian Rogers (South Africa)		

Denis McBride replaced by Eddie Halvey
John Davies replaced by Ricky Evans

GAME PROGRESSION
field possession / time

T: POPPLEWELL C: ELWOOD 7-0
T: McBRIDE C: ELWOOD 14-0
◄ PG: JENKINS 14-3
◄ DG: DAVIES 14-6

14 HALF TIME 06

◄ DG: JENKINS 14-9
T: HALVEY C: ELWOOD 21-9
T: HUMPHREYS C: JENKINS 21-16
PG: ELWOOD 24-16 ►
T: TAYLOR C: JENKINS 24-23

FINAL SCORE
24 • 23

MAN OF THE MATCH: DENIS McBRIDE

With an elusive weave to the left, Anthony Clement kicks downfield. It was a brave fight back by the Welsh reds against the Irish greens that ended in a one point difference.

Robert Jones passes the ball before the onslaught of big Irishman Nick Popplewell.

ENGLAND vs WEST SAMOA

DURBAN • 4 JUNE • 20:00

By the end the pristine King's Park surface was littered with so many battered and bleeding bodies it resembled a medieval battlefield more than a rugby pitch. A confrontation bar none had been promised between the South Sea warriors and the men manning the English ramparts - and for those who like their rugby on the "rare" side, this was a real feast.

The English management selected a mix-and-match team to take on a Samoan side deprived through injury to a couple of their shining lights, Darren Kellet and Junior Paramore.

The match was significant for the return to action of England's forward, no. 8 Dean Richards, who had been sidelined by hamstring trouble. It took Richards just 60 seconds to make his considerable presence felt. After marshalling England's first truly dynamic driving maul of the tournament to carry play to the Samoan line, he shepherded flanker Neil Back over on the blind-side.

The English didn't look back. The pack used its big guns to good effect to turn the screw and two Jonathan Callard penalties, a Mike Catt drop-goal, and a Rory Underwood try just before the break gave them a 21 - 0 half-time lead.

Despite the scoreline, the Samoans were far from being overwhelmed and the ferocity of the first-half combat saw England's Back and Rowntree and Samoa's Leevasa and Puleitu retire injured.

The introduction of Feta Sini at fly-half for Puleitu at half-time provided the spark the Samoans needed when, after an exchange of penalties between Callard and Faamaino, the stocky "super-sub" ricocheted his way through the English defence twice for tries from tap-penalties.

With their points cushion reduced to an uncomfortable 24 - 17, the English forwards responded with a storming drive that was rewarded with a penalty try against the Samoans for deliberately collapsing the maul. This was augmented by a further Callard penalty and a slick second try for Rory Underwood and the game was effectively over bar the numerous comings and goings - England eventually using five replacements and the Samoans four - and a late try by Mika Umaga.

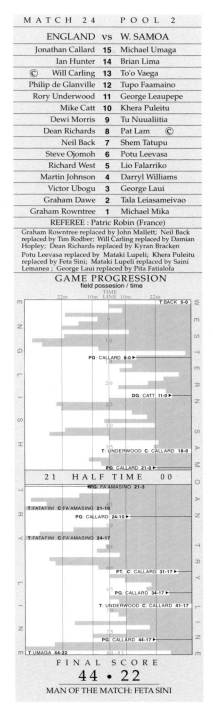

MATCH 24		POOL 2
ENGLAND	vs	W. SAMOA
Jonathan Callard	15	Michael Umaga
Ian Hunter	14	Brian Lima
© Will Carling	13	To'o Vaega
Philip de Glanville	12	Tupo Faamaino
Rory Underwood	11	George Leaupepe
Mike Catt	10	Khera Puleitu
Dewi Morris	9	Tu Nuualiitia
Dean Richards	8	Pat Lam ©
Neil Back	7	Shem Tatupu
Steve Ojomoh	6	Potu Leevasa
Richard West	5	Lio Falarriko
Martin Johnson	4	Darryl Williams
Victor Ubogu	3	George Laui
Graham Dawe	2	Tala Leiasameivao
Graham Rowntree	1	Michael Mika

REFEREE : Patric Robin (France)

Graham Rowntree replaced by John Mallett; Neil Back replaced by Tim Rodber; Will Carling replaced by Damian Hopley; Dean Richards replaced by Kyran Bracken Potu Leevasa replaced by Mataki Lupeli; Khera Puleitu replaced by Feta Sini; Mataki Lupeli replaced by Saini Lemanea ; George Laui replaced by Pita Fatialofa

GAME PROGRESSION
field possesion / time

TIME
22m 10m LINE 10m 22m

T.BACK 5-0
PG: CALLARD 6-0 ►
DG: CATT 11-0 ►
T: UNDERWOOD C: CALLARD 18-0 ►
PG: CALLARD 21-0 ►

21 HALF TIME 00

PG: FA'AMASINO 21-3
T:FATAFINI C:FA'AMASINO 21-10
PG: CALLARD 24-10 ►
T:FATAFINI C:FA'AMASINO 24-17
PT. C: CALLARD 31-17 ►
PG: CALLARD 34-17 ►
T: UNDERWOOD C: CALLARD 41-17 ►
PG: CALLARD 44-17 ►
T:UMAGA 44-22

FINAL SCORE
44 • 22

MAN OF THE MATCH: FETA SINI

In a feast of rugby, rich in spectator appeal and hard fought territory, it was the brilliance of men like Mike Catt that made the English win so memorable.

Tim Rodber, coming on as a replacement, clears the ball to the receptive hands of Steve Ojomoh.

FRANCE vs IRELAND

DURBAN • 10 JUNE • 13:00

The motto of the French Foreign Legion is "March or Die" - and in this Durban quarter-final, coach Pierre Berbizier's side marched right over a strangely subdued Ireland.

Irish hopes were, ultimately, trampled into the sun-baked Natal turf through a combined assault by the big French pack and a magnificent goal-kicking display by centre Thierry Lacroix, who finished the match with eight penalties.

France prevailed, as they have every time the sides have met in the Five Nations since 1983, mainly because the Irish pack was unable to cope with the assault of the dominant French eight. Lacroix, meanwhile, established a record-equalling performance in penalty points-gathering.

Initially the match was something of a damp squib, and, in a half-empty King's Park, you could have been forgiven for wondering whether there really was a World Cup quarter-final at stake. All the pre-match threats of fire and brimstone, from Ireland in particular, fizzled out in the first-half as two tentative teams fumbled their way to a 12 - 12 stalemate at the interval, Irish fly-half Eric Elwood matching Lacroix kick for kick.

Set against their rampaging first-half against the All Blacks and explosive beginning against Wales, the Irish were a pale imitation of their former selves. Nor were the French, given their near total domination of the line-outs through Roumat, Benazzi and Cabannes, their usual sparkling selves with the halfback pairing of Hueber and Deylaud symptomatic of their lack of incisiveness.

After the break, however, the French forwards, with Merle, Benazzi, Cecillon and Roumat to the fore, began to rumble and Irish resistance - with the notable exception of Corkery upfront and a back-line that tackled its weight - began to crumble.

The pressure told and Lacroix landed four further penalties to give the French an unassailable 24 - 12 lead. Then, a minute before full-time, captain Phillippe Saint Andre compounded Irish misery by stealing through for the first try of the match. Not to be outdone, fellow winger Emile Ntamack intercepted a Brendan Mullin pass on his own 22 to score four minutes into injury time, consigning Ireland to a resounding third successive quarter-final defeat.

Man of the match, Thierry Lacroix, in devastating form and with decisive kicks for goal, keeps the scoreboard adding up for a win for France.

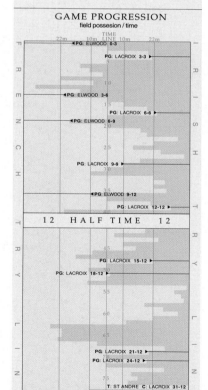

GAME 24	QUARTER FINAL	
FRANCE	vs	IRELAND
Jean-Luc Sadourny	15	Conor O'Shea
Emile Ntamack	14	Darrach O'Mahony
Phillippe Sella	13	Brendan Mullin
Thierry Lacroix	12	Jonathan Bell
© Phillippe Saint Andre	11	Simon Geoghegan
Christophe Deylaud	10	Eric Elwood
Aubin Hueber	9	Niall Hogan
Marc Cecillon	8	Paddy Johns
Laurent Cabannes	7	Denis McBride
Abdelatif Benazzi	6	David Corkery
Olivier Roumat	5	Neil Francis
Olivier Merle	4	Gabriel Fulcher
Christian Califano	3	Gary Halpin
Jean-Michel Gonzalez	2	Terry Kingston ©
Louis Armary	1	Nick Popplewell
REFEREE : Ed Morrison (England)		

Gabriel Fulcher replaced by Eddie Halvey

GAME PROGRESSION
field possession / time

◄ PG: ELWOOD 0-3

PG: LACROIX 3-3 ►

◄ PG: ELWOOD 3-6

PG: LACROIX 6-6 ►

◄ PG: ELWOOD 6-9

PG: LACROIX 9-9 ►

◄ PG: ELWOOD 9-12

PG: LACROIX 12-12 ►

12   HALF TIME   12

PG: LACROIX 15-12 ►

PG: LACROIX 18-12 ►

PG: LACROIX 21-12 ►

PG: LACROIX 24-12 ►

T: ST ANDRE C: LACROIX 31-12

T: NTAMACK 36-12

FINAL SCORE
36 • 12

MAN OF THE MATCH: THIERRY LACROIX

Centre Brendan Mullin Breaks from his props, Garrett Halpin and Nick Popplewell.

Ntamack intercepts the Irish ball, runs a spectacular eighty metres and seals the match for France with a try.

Gabriel Fulcher brings the line out ball down for Ireland; Auburn Heuber clears for France with a dive pass.

SOUTH AFRICA
vs WEST SAMOA

JOHANNESBURG • 10 JUNE • 15:30

Chester Williams was back in town. The flying Springbok left wing, charismatic darling of rugby journalists, in his first World Cup match, raced into the South African record books as the first Springbok to score four tries in a Test match. It was a Boys' Own tale of triumph after disappointment as Williams returned to the South African side after withdrawing before the tournament owing to a hamstring injury. And how the crowd loved him!

But the joy of victory was tempered by a bruising encounter that saw serious injuries to key players: Andre Joubert (hand), Ruben Kruger (shoulder), Mark Andrews (rib) and Kobus Wiese (knee). [*See statistics panel.*]

The Western Samoans were guilty of some gross stiff-arm and late tackles and were lucky not to have to pay more than the price of penalties for their indiscretions. Mika Umaga was later suspended for 60 days. The penalty count of 22 - 8 in favour of the Springboks gives a graphic indication of the Western Samoans' disregard for even the basic proprieties of rugby football.

Their never-say-die commitment did however bring some impressive second-half running. The try scored by lively scrum-half Tu Nuualiitia was a great surge as South Africa attacked the Western Samoan line. The Samoans came up the left-hand touch line, lost the ball in a tackle then regained from a tackle on Gavin Johnson and raced down for Nuualiitia's dive over Japie Mulder's tackle. That movement probably travelled two lengths of a rugby field.

The game was a running spectacle that kept the large Ellis Park crowd in a state of constant excitement. In addition to Chester Williams, Mark Andrews and Chris Rossouw crossed for tries, while Gavin Johnson weighed in with three conversions and two penalties. The Springbok forwards were impressive and their control of the line-outs, scrums and mauls for most of the game paved the way for victory.

It was a great day for South Africa who advance to play France in the semi-final. But there was a price to pay.

Chester Williams in his first appearance in the tournament runs in four tries in the match and creates a new South African record.

GAME 26   QUARTER FINAL

SOUTH AFRICA		vs	WEST SAMOA
Andre Joubert	15		Mika Umaga
Gavin Johnson	14		Brian Lima
Christiaan Scholtz	13		To'o Vaega
Japie Mulder	12		Tupo Faamaino
Chester Williams	11		George Harder
Hennie le Roux	10		Feta Sini
Joost vd Westhuizen	9		Tu Nuualiitia
Rudolph Straeuli	8		Pat Lam ⓒ
Ruben Kruger	7		Junior Paramore
ⓒ Francois Pienaar	6		Shem Tatupu
Mark Andrews	5		Lio Falarriko
Kobus Wiese	4		Saini Lemanea
Balie Swart	3		George Laui
Chris Rossouw	2		Tala Leiasameivao
Pieter du Randt	1		Michael Mika

REFEREE : Jim Fleming (Scotland)

Andre Joubert replaced by Brendan Venter; Ruben Kruger replaced by Adriaan Richter; Mark Andrews replaced by Krynauw Otto; Kobus Wiese replaced by Naka Drotske George Harder replaced by Fereti Tuilagi; George Laui replaced by Pita Fatialofa; Mike Mika replaced by Brendan Reily; Junior Paramore replaced by Sila Viafale.

GAME PROGRESSION
field possession / time

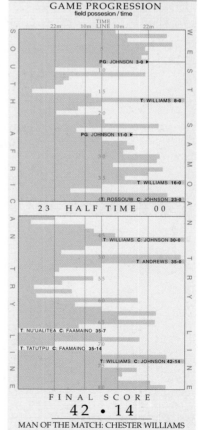

PG: JOHNSON 3-0 ▶

T: WILLIAMS 8-0

PG: JOHNSON 11-0 ▶

T: WILLIAMS 16-0

T: ROSSOUW C: JOHNSON 23-0

23   HALF TIME   00

T: WILLIAMS C: JOHNSON 30-0

T: ANDREWS 35-0

T: NU'UALITEA C: FAAMAINO 35-7

T: TATUTPU C: FAAMAINO 35-14

T: WILLIAMS C: JOHNSON 42-14

FINAL SCORE
42 • 14

MAN OF THE MATCH: CHESTER WILLIAMS

Slipping out of the Samoans' reach, Chester Williams runs on to become our Man of the Match.

Tu Nuualiitia flings the ball far from his hefty pack.

Any Springbok is fair game for a solid encounter: Japie Mulder; Francois Pienaar; Joost van der Westhuizen.

It's a crushing victory as Chester Williams, with ear to the ground, wrestles against mighty odds to put the ball down for a try.

ENGLAND
vs AUSTRALIA

NEWLANDS • 11 JUNE • 13:00

England expected ... and Rob Andrew delivered: his booming 40-metre drop-goal two minutes into extra time settled this titanic struggle and turned the Wallabies into ex-world champions. It could not have been more thrillingly scripted and it was one of the most remarkable climaxes to a match ever witnessed.

With extra time beckoning, the England fly-half kept his cool to hammer the ball between the uprights. Australian captain Michael Lynagh, though devastated, was characteristically gracious despite seeing his side's much heralded "Operation Repeat" transformed into operation defeat.

Lynagh, whose own near immaculate goal-kicking haul of five penalties and a conversion almost clinched it for the Wallabies, described Andrew's match-winning effort as "a fantastic kick in circumstances of extraordinary pressure".

The England hero, who matched Lynagh penalty for penalty, commented: "It was textbook stuff. Penalty, line-out, drive, drop-goal. A great catch and drive by Martin Bayfield was taken up by the forwards and it gave me the chance. I struck it well, it was flying ..." It certainly was - and so was the rest of the England camp as referee David Bishop blew for time. Ultimately England deserved their nail-biting win, not just for the manner in which they subdued the Wallabies for much of the first-half but for the way they came back at the death after Australia, nursing a 22 - 19 lead, had seemingly shut them out in a pulsating final quarter.

England, leading 6 - 3 through two Andrew penalties to Lynagh's one, took a commanding 13 - 3 lead midway through the first half when Andrew swooped on the ball spilled by the usually reliable Lynagh for Guscott and Carling to combine, before putting winger Tony Underwood away from 50 metres for a scorching try.

However, a Wallaby fightback, begun immediately after the interval with a spectacular Damian Smith try resulting from a brilliant airborne catch, levelled the score. With the Australian pack edging out the big English eight, and John Eales playing superbly, Lynagh stole a march - but Andrew, through a late penalty and that drop-goal, stole the show.

GAME 27 QUARTER FINAL

ENGLAND	vs	AUSTRALIA
Mike Catt	15	Matthew Burke
Tony Underwood	14	Damian Smith
© Will Carling	13	Jason Little
Jeremy Guscott	12	Tim Horan
Rory Underwood	11	David Campese
Rob Andrew	10	Michael Lynagh ©
Dewi Morris	9	George Gregan
Dean Richards	8	Tim Gavin
Ben Clarke	7	David Wilson
Tim Rodber	6	Willie Ofahengaue
Martin Bayfield	5	John Eales
Martin Johnson	4	Rod McCall
Victor Ubogu	3	Ewan McKenzie
Brian Moore	2	Phillip Kearnes
Jason Leonard	1	Dan Crowley

REFEREE : David Bishop (New Zealand)

Dean Richards replaced by Steve Ojomoh

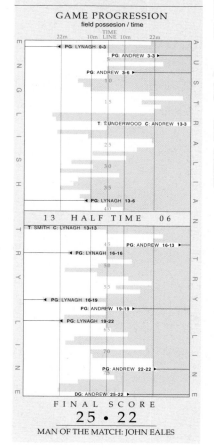

GAME PROGRESSION
field possesion / time

PG: LYNAGH 0-3
PG: ANDREW 3-3
PG: ANDREW 3-6
T: T.UNDERWOOD C: ANDREW 13-3
PG: LYNAGH 13-6

13 HALF TIME 06

T: SMITH C: LYNAGH 13-13
PG: ANDREW 16-13
PG: LYNAGH 16-16
PG: LYNAGH 16-19
PG: ANDREW 19-19
PG: LYNAGH 19-22
PG: ANDREW 22-22
DG: ANDREW 25-22

FINAL SCORE
25 • 22

MAN OF THE MATCH: JOHN EALES

The Kick: Time has run out. The scores are level. The ball flies to Andrew. He kicks at goal. All eyes watch the flight of the ball except Rob Andrew, a surveyor, who needs no theodolite to tell us its line is true.

The End: Campese and Underwood leave the field, but never will anyone forget the drama of this titanic contest.

The Struggle: Unrelenting, like Greek gods fighting for the marbles of Zeus, Tim Horan, Mike Catt and Will Carling give everything to change the destiny of that ball.

The Try: In a scene from Aussie Rules, Damian Smith plucks the ball clean out of the sky... to an audible gasp from the Newlands crowd, which turns to a roar as he crashes to the ground, rolls over the tryline and levels the score: 13-13.

The Run: Tony Underwood beats the tackle that nearly put his foot out of touch, then races downfield for a try.

The Effort: Nobody, in this Herculean struggle, has a moment to relax. And nobody gives more than Dewi Morris.

NEW ZEALAND vs SCOTLAND

PRETORIA • 11 JUNE • 15:30

At last, at this tournament a team emerged to prove that the New Zealanders were human after all, and that they could be forced into errors under pressure from committed defenders. Scotland's determination and belief that they could bring off an upset was apparent from the kickoff as they flew into the rucks and mauls and tackled the All Blacks behind the advantage line.

Not that the All Blacks, now playing for the first time in South Africa in white jerseys, appeared in danger of losing to a team that had never beaten them. The Scottish defence was found wanting at a crucial stage of the second half when the weight and drive of the New Zealanders ruthlessly exploited some weak tackling and led to tries. The measure of New Zealand's superiority was the six tries to three advantage when the final whistle blew.

In the end the difference between the two sides was that Scotland had no answer to the penetrative running of the New Zealand backs. The likes of Bachop, Mehrtens (who showed a winger's pace for his 70 metre try), Little (two tries), Bunce and Lomu (one try each) seemed to be able to break the line at will. Fitzpatrick made the other try.

Scotland's Craig Joiner had the daunting job of marking Lomu who has yet to find an opponent able to contain him. He does not score every time he gets the ball, but it takes so many defenders to bring him down that supporting All Blacks ranging up on his shoulder are able to cross the try line unmarked.

Scotland was always in the game. Two spectacularly long Hastings kicks at goal from the halfway mark went home. Doddie Weir became the second player to score two tries in a match against the All Blacks at this tournament. Scott Hastings scored the third. Scotland scored 30 points against the All Blacks (only Australia, back in 1978, has done that before).

Gavin Hastings, playing in his last game for Scotland, exceeding 100 points for the tournament, led a fine performance by his team. Every player walked proudly from the game.

The New Zealanders, in unfamiliar Black and White, open with the Haka as Hastings's men stand resolute. Jeff Wilson in flight; Jonah Lomu is unsinkable.

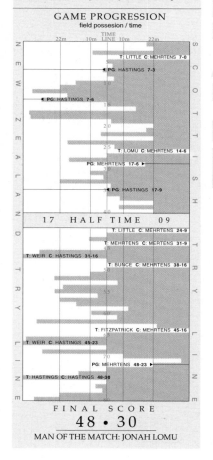

GAME 28   QUARTER FINAL

NEW ZEALAND	vs	SCOTLAND
Jeff Wilson	15	Gavin Hastings ©
Marc Ellis	14	Craig Joiner
Frank Bunce	13	Scott Hastings
Walter Little	12	Andrew Shiel
Jonah Lomu	11	Kenny Logan
Andrew Mehrtens	10	Craig Chalmers
Graeme Bachop	9	Bryan Redpath
Zinzan Brooke	8	Eric Peters
Josh Kronfeld	7	Iain Morrison
Jamie Joseph	6	Rob Wainwright
Robin Brooke	5	Doddie Weir
Ian Jones	4	Damian Cronin
Olo Brown	3	Peter Wright
© Sean Fitzpatrick	2	Kenny Milne
Richard Loe	1	David Hilton

REFEREE : Derek Bevan (Wales)

Craig Chalmers replaced by Ian Jardine
Damian Cronin replaced by Stewart Campbell

GAME PROGRESSION
field possession / time

T: LITTLE C: MEHRTENS 7-0
PG: HASTINGS 7-3
PG: HASTINGS 7-6
T: LOMU C: MEHRTENS 14-6
PG: MEHRTENS 17-6
PG: HASTINGS 17-9

17   HALF TIME   09

T: LITTLE C: MEHRTENS 24-9
T: MEHRTENS C: MERTENS 31-9
T: WEIR C: HASTINGS 31-16
T: BUNCE C: MEHRTENS 38-16
T: FITZPATRICK C: MEHRTENS 45-16
T: WEIR C: HASTINGS 45-23
PG: MEHRTENS 48-23
T: HASTINGS C: HASTINGS 48-30

FINAL SCORE
48 • 30

MAN OF THE MATCH: JONAH LOMU

Gavin Hastings throws everything into this, his last game for Scotland.

Andrew Mehrtens claims 23 points with two penalty goals, six conversions and a long sprint to the line for a try.

Marc Ellis is brought to the ground by a gritty Scottish defence.

The nutcracker movement of Josh Kronfeld, in headgear, and Frank Bunce, tightens on Scotland's Craig Chalmers.

Jonah Lomu on the charge on legs like Kauri pine trunks. Perhaps the time has come for the nation's mascot of a shy Kiwi to be replaced by the Moa, New Zealand's ancient, giant bird.

SOUTH AFRICA vs FRANCE

DURBAN • 17 JUNE • 16:30

Monsoon! Durban was swamped by a tropical downpour for most of the day. It did not, however, douse the spirits of two sides that produced an ebb-and-flow contest of huge endeavour and buckets of courage.

That South Africa eventually emerged triumphant from the Durban deluge to stake a claim to the final at Ellis Park was due not only to their ability to adapt to the swimming-pool conditions in the first half but also to their refusal to allow burning ambition to be doused by the extraordinary pre-match drama: the teams had to endure an unprecedented 90 minute delay. Concerns not only of injury to the players but also of a lightning strike left the administrators in limbo. It was left to Welsh referee Derek Bevan to decide whether or not he considered that the binding scrummagers would survive a collapsed scrum with their faces submerged in water.

At stake was not simply a disruption to the World Cup schedule but the possibility that, should the weather not improve for a replay the following day, South Africa could go tumbling out of the competition because the French would have gone through to the final on the strength of a superior disciplinary record (the Springboks carried the baggage of the higher number of citings and sendings-off in the tournament). Ironically, the delay coincided almost exactly with the only part of the day in which the rain actually abated. No sooner did Bevan finally get the proceedings underway than the heavens opened again.

The Springboks started with such steely intent that it seemed not even the sheets of rain would blur their focus on the Webb Ellis Trophy. A first-minute penalty by fly-half Joel Stransky following a quicksilver break by scrumhalf Joost van der Westhuizen from a short line-out tap by Mark Andrews, shifted from lock to no. 8 by coach Christie, set the Springboks on their way. The opening quarter of the match belonged to South Africa, despite early indications that the French were prepared to run. When French powerhouse Olivier Merle carried the ball into contact, twice it emerged like a bar of soap on the Springbok side of the ruck. But where France

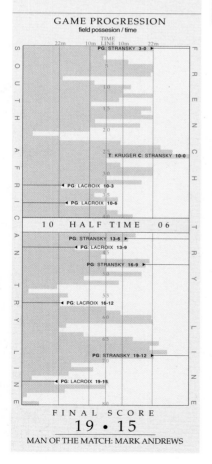

MATCH 29		SEMI-FINAL
SOUTH AFRICA	vs	FRANCE
Andre Joubert	15	Jean-Luc Sadourny
James Small	14	Emile Ntamack
Japie Mulder	13	Phillippe Sella
Hennie Le Roux	12	Thierry Lacroix
Chester Williams	11	Phillippe Saint Andre ©
Joel Stransky	10	Christophe Deylaud
Joost vd Westhuizen	9	Fabien Galchie
Mark Andrews	8	Marc Cecillon
Ruben Kruger	7	Laurent Cabannes
© Francois Pienaar	6	Abdelatif Benazzi
Hannes Strydom	5	Olivier Roumat
Kobus Wiese	4	Olivier Merle
Balie Swart	3	Christian Califano
Chris Rossouw	2	Jean-Michel Gonzalez
Pieter Du Randt	1	Louis Armary
REFEREE : Derek Bevan (Wales)		

Joost vd Westhuizen replaced by Johan Roux

GAME PROGRESSION
field possesion / time

PG: STRANSKY 3-0 ►

T: KRUGER C: STRANSKY 10-0

◄ PG: LACROIX 10-3

◄ PG: LACROIX 10-6

10 HALF TIME 06

PG: STRANSKY 13-6 ►

◄ PG: LACROIX 13-9

PG: STRANSKY 16-9 ►

◄ PG: LACROIX 16-12

PG: STRANSKY 19-12 ►

◄ PG: LACROIX 19-15

FINAL SCORE
19 • 15
MAN OF THE MATCH: MARK ANDREWS

It was a game of mud and guts, but nothing (neither drenching storm, nor relentless French attack, nor injured hand) could erode Andre Joubert's rock solid defence.

The 90 minute storm-delayed start brought on heightened tensions and water sweepers.

was inclined to be more profligate with their possession, the Springbok watchword was "control". Spearheaded by burly flanker Ruben Kruger, one of the outstanding forwards in the Springbok eight, the South Africans were the more cohesive of the two packs. In addition, the South African kicking - with both Joubert and Stransky showing great composure - was more astute than that of their opposites, Sadourny and Deylaud.

With the territorial balance in their favour, the Springboks were rewarded with what proved to be a crucial score 25 minutes into the half. Another Andrews deflection from the front of a line-out saw van der Westhuizen make a telling break to carry play to a few metres from the French line. Wiese and Kruger spun off the maul for the flanker to twist over the line to register the only try of the match.

After Stransky was unable to build on the 10 - 0 lead, missing a difficult penalty, France came back strongly with their excellent backrow of Cabannes, Benazzi and Cecillon to the fore. Injudicious backchat to referee Bevan by the Springboks advanced two penalties to within striking distance for Lacroix to cut the Springbok lead to 10 - 6 at half-time.

With the second half turning into a real water-polo scramble, France made headway in attack, with Ntamack and Saint Andre a persistent threat to Springbok hopes. However, they failed to match South Africa's discipline at the breakdown, and after an opening exchange of penalties between Stransky and Lacroix, Stransky struck again to give the Springboks a 16 - 9 lead going into the final quarter.

The French, seeing their World Cup dream ebbing away, redoubled their efforts. A Lacroix penalty followed, only to be nullified when a Merle head butt on Pienaar saw Stransky hit the target to keep South Africa 19 - 12 ahead.

Still France came at the Springboks. With five minutes remaining, the deadly accurate Lacroix stroked home his fifth penalty, 19 - 15. In a frenzied final few minutes the French kicked up the spray as they hammered at the line knowing that one try would do it. And they came within a hand span of achieving it when Benazzi, following a Deylaud up-and-under, slipped. Otherwise, size and momentum, despite the presence of James Small, must have carried him over.

An afternoon of high drama ended with the French camped on the South African line, striving in vain for a pushover try. But the Springbok defence held firm - as it had all afternoon - and the Umbrella Test was theirs.

Position is possession as Stydom takes the ball from the lineout to van der Westhuizen.

Wonderful weather for frogs: soaked to the core, Berzier tries to power his way past the Springbok defence.

As Fabien Galchie crashes off Joost van der Westhuizen, a spray of steam from body heat, perspiration and rain soaked jersey explodes off his shoulders.

Stransky, in cool control, passes a tight ball to Joubert; a mighty driving Springbok effort is rewarded by a try.

Tenacious defence to the gut-wrenching end as Le Roux clears a low, tight ball back over the tryline. A dropped ball would spell disaster in the last few seconds of the game.

That's it! Final whistle and Pienaar's men have held out.

NEW ZEALAND vs ENGLAND

NEWLANDS • 18 JUNE • 15:00

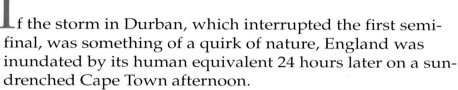

If the storm in Durban, which interrupted the first semi-final, was something of a quirk of nature, England was inundated by its human equivalent 24 hours later on a sun-drenched Cape Town afternoon.

Jonah Lomu, the 20-year-old, 1,95m, 118kg All Black left wing of Tongan parentage, was the harbinger of the havoc. Despite the brave words beforehand from the England camp about putting the youngster under pressure, the tables were turned right after the kick-off. Lomu, bearing down on Tony Underwood and Will Carling, harried them into conceding a scrum after they had botched Andrew Mehrtens' switched kick-off, and he subsequently latched onto a long loose ball 30 metres from the English line.

Sensationally handing off Tony Underwood's challenge, the massive Lomu rode a Carling ankle-tap before running straight over the hapless Mike Catt to score an irresistible opening try. The game was barely two minutes old. England looked stunned. The wheels had not so much come off their chariot at Newlands as had been smashed off. And that was just the beginning.

Two minutes later New Zealand struck the "killer" blow after Walter Little knifed through the English midfield from deep within his own half. He and Glen Osborne exchanged passes, Osborne providing the scoring pass for ever-present flanker Josh Kronfeld. Mehrtens converted and, with the English shell-shocked by the sheer speed and ferocity of the New Zealand assault, no. 8 Zinzan Brooke added insult to injury by slamming over a superb opportunist drop-goal from 45 metres, giving the All Blacks an 18 - 0 lead midway through the first half.

The rout of the Five Nations champions was made complete when, 15 minutes before half time, Lomu struck again. Set up by a Jeff Wilson blind-side break and huge cross-field pass by Zinzan Brooke, Lomu swept imperiously past Rob Andrew on his way to the line.

Despite the experience of players such as Rob Andrew, Brian Moore and Dean Richards, England was unable to get

MATCH 30		SEMI-FINAL
NEW ZEALAND	vs	ENGLAND
Glen Osborne	15	Mike Catt
Jeff Wilson	14	Tony Underwood
Frank Bunce	13	Will Carling ⓒ
Walter Little	12	Jeremy Guscott
Jonah Lomu	11	Rory Underwood
Andrew Mehrtens	10	Rob Andrew
Graeme Bachop	9	Dewi Morris
Zinzan Brooke	8	Dean Richards
Josh Kronfeld	7	Ben Clarke
Michael Brewer	6	Tim Rodber
Robin Brooke	5	Martin Bayfield
Ian Jones	4	Martin Johnson
Olo Brown	3	Victor Ubogu
ⓒ Sean Fitzpatrick	2	Brian Moore
Craig Dowd	1	Jason Leonard

REFEREE : Stephen Hilditch (Ireland)

Zinzan Brooke replaced by Blair Larson

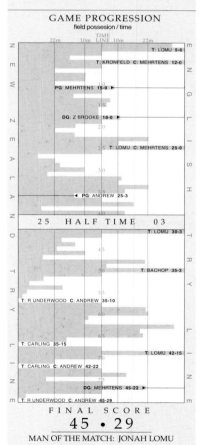

GAME PROGRESSION
field possesion / time

T: LOMU 5-0

T: KRONFELD C: MEHRTENS 12-0

PG: MEHRTENS 15-0 ▶

DG: Z BROOKE 18-0

T: LOMU C: MEHRTENS 25-0

◀ PG: ANDREW 25-3

25   HALF TIME   03

T: LOMU 30-3

T: BACHOP 35-3

T: R UNDERWOOD C: ANDREW 35-10

T: CARLING 35-15

T: LOMU 42-15

T: CARLING C: ANDREW 42-22

DG: MEHRTENS 45-22 ▶

T: R UNDERWOOD C: ANDREW 45-29

FINAL SCORE
45 • 29

MAN OF THE MATCH: JONAH LOMU

Looming larger than life, the locomotive-like Lomu lopes to the line. It was a devastating start that left England asking how to stop him; and as they adopted the motto "If at first you don't succeed …" Lomu responded with try, try, try, try again.

New Zealand's on the loose as Walter Little slips neatly out of Jeremy Guscott's arms.

to grips with the pace and adventure of the All Blacks. Their pre-match intention of throttling the New Zealand pack never materialised. Ian Jones and Robin Brooke proved more than a match for England's tall men at the line-out, while Craig Dowd gave Victor Ubogu an uncomfortable afternoon at the scrummage. As for the loose, the All Blacks seemed a metre faster in both thought and deed, leaving the big English pack trailing in its wake. Their backs fared even worse. Noted in the past for solid defence, their "first-up" tackling was woefully deficient. Their demise was anticipated by Rob Andrew's change in fortunes.

It is said that a week is a long time in politics, but Andrew will tell you it is nothing compared with a week in rugby. England's drop-goal hero against Australia could not put a foot right. Two penalties and a drop-goal went begging and then, to rub salt in the wound, he spilled the ball as England mounted their first threatening attack of the match. Hitting the target with a penalty just before the interval was scant consolation. With the score at 25 - 3, the game had probably already been won and lost.

Just as Lomu had left his huge, indelible imprint on the first half, so too did he in the second. One minute was all it took as, from a Jones line-out, Little and Kronfeld combined to give Lomu, whose sheer speed and balance for such a big man was extraordinary, his hat trick. Ten minutes later the All Blacks rammed home their superiority when Graeme Bachop instigated and then scored from a superbly executed backrow move off a scrum on the English 10 metre line to establish a 35 - 3 lead.

England, in danger of being totally humiliated, salvaged some pride from the wreckage in the final quarter. Rory Underwood began the fightback by squeezing in at the corner - even though television replays showed he had been forced into touch. With Ben Clarke taking the ball up the middle, England at last found some shape. Carling capitalised on the space by running in two tries, the first from a neatly judged touch-line chip and gather. In between, however, Lomu was the beneficiary of England's belated attempts to spin the ball, scoring his fourth try from a Bachop intercept.

England brought some respectability to the score line when Rory Underwood scored his second on the stroke of time. This enabled the Five Nations champions to salvage some pride by outscoring the All Blacks by four tries to three in the second half, but it was scant compensation and failed to redress the all-round superiority of the New Zealanders.

Carling is caught.
Ubogu is unceremoniously upended.

Will Carling's skillful chip ahead deflects off Lomu and back into Carling's hands as he passes his obstacle and runs in a try.

In a sprint to the line, Underwood beats Lomu to score a try for England.

Robin Brooke takes the lineout; Underwood takes a stand against Osborne; Catt takes Osborne out of touch.

No man is an island, particulary in a team sport, but four tries brings up the Lomu tally to 20 more points to set him apart in this encounter. Whilst Jonah was erupting into world headlines in South Africa, a new volcano emerged out of the South Pacific giving his homeland, Tonga, its 151st possession. It has been officially named Lomu Island.

FRANCE vs ENGLAND

PRETORIA • 22 JUNE • 17:00

With the managements of both sides questioning the wisdom of a third-place play-off, the writing was on the wall that this match might not be a classic.

The pre-match pessimism proved to be well founded, but France's more competitive semi-final performance made it the side more likely to rise to the occasion.

While for the match winner there was the incentive of automatic qualification for the 1999 tournament, France was also motivated to avenge eight successive defeats at the hands of England.

That the Tricolors ultimately achieved that end, scoring two fine second-half tries in the process, spoke more of England's almost total absence of ambition than it did of an overdose of French flair. The English players seemed totally devoid of attacking ideas.

With fly-half Rob Andrew and fullback Mike Catt opting for the up-and-under and the kick to touch as their main means of attack, it took most of the first half before England finally began to move the ball along the line.

Despite the English taking the lead with an Andrew penalty just before the half-hour, the more adventurous French were beginning to get England's measure. This was particularly true in the forwards where the French tight five had the English scrummage creaking and in the loose with Abdelatif Benazzi and Laurent Cabannes in fine fettle.

France was rewarded right at the end of the half when a Thierry Lacroix penalty levelled the score at 3 - 3.

After the interval, Lacroix and Andrew exchanged further penalties before Lacroix, who, with a total of 112, finished as the tournament's top points scorer, put France ahead 9 - 6 going into the final quarter. The French pack then clinched the match when they formed a driving maul from a line-out for the excellent Olivier Roumat to force his way over.

Adrift 14 - 6, England made a belated attempt to open up but, despite a third Andrew penalty and a gutsy display by Dewi Morris, the French defence held firm. Two minutes from time, the lethal Emile Ntamack beat three English tacklers to end France's World Cup campaign with a flourish.

MATCH 31   PLAY-OFF

FRANCE	vs	ENGLAND
Jean-Luc Sadourny	15	Mike Catt
Emile Ntamack	14	Ian Hunter
Phillippe Sella	13	Will Carling ©
Thierry Lacroix	12	Jeremy Guscott
© Phillippe Saint Andre	11	Rory Underwood
Franck Mesnel	10	Rob Andrew
Fabien Galthie	9	Dewi Morris
Albert Cigagna	8	Steve Ojomoh
Laurent Cabannes	7	Ben Clarke
Abdelatif Benazzi	6	Tim Rodber
Olivier Roumat	5	Martin Bayfield
Olivier Merle	4	Martin Johnson
Christian Califano	3	Victor Ubogu
Jean-Michel Gonzalez	2	Brian Moore
Laurent Benezech	1	Jason Leonard

REFEREE : David Bishop (New Zealand)

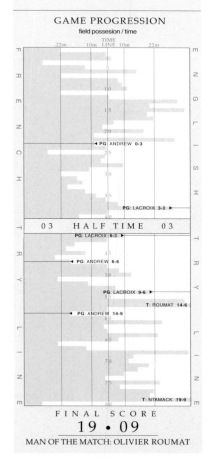

GAME PROGRESSION
field possesion / time

FINAL SCORE
19 • 09

MAN OF THE MATCH: OLIVIER ROUMAT

Abdelatif Benazzi flies through the English defence of Rob Andrew and Steve Ojomoh. After a stalemated first-half, the French Legionnaires take more territory.

Despite British bulldog tenacity, Rob Andrew (now MBE), finds the tail feathers of the French cock Jean-Luc Sadourny.

If work rate alone could win matches, Dewi Morris would have put England ahead, but France, with more diverse play, wins the day and automatic enrtry to the next Rugby World Cup.

The International Rugby Football Board
The Webb Ellis Cup

THE
FINAL

Rugby World Cup 1995 has already become the greatest rugby tournament ever held, no matter who wins the trophy today.

South Africa can stand proud. For the new democracy, its people, its warmth of hospitality, its organisational skills, its facilities and the re-emergence of the Springboks have all contributed greatly to the character and success of these games.

This month of contests will be well remembered for the great courage, skill, talent and effort, the drama, the spectator appeal, the painted faces, the roar of the crowd, the camaraderie and goodwill fostered among nations through person-to-person contact and, more so, as the start of a new era.

The old principles of amateurism that lasted a hundred years will be gone at the top ranks and the effects will surely filter down. No longer can Rugby Union expect its youth to sacrifice careers for sport; sport will become their career.

It will be four years before the next Rugby World Cup. May we all meet again in Wales in 1999.

Dr Tony O'Reilly

By all measures, and acknowledged by the world's critics, the enormous Ellis Park, with its big crowd capacity, with more than 400 corporate suites, excellent playing conditions, player and press facilities, rates as one of the greatest stadia in the world.

SOUTH AFRICA vs NEW ZEALAND

ELLIS PARK • 24 JUNE • 15:00

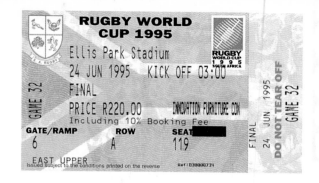

On the eve of the Rugby World Cup Final the headlines gave the bombshell news of a multimillion rand deal for Rugby Union. The R2 billion (US$ 550 million) package over 10 years, announced jointly by Rupert Murdoch, Louis Luyt, Richie Guy and Leo Williams, will establish a SANZA tournament to bring the southern hemisphere giants, South Africa, New Zealand and Australia, into annual competition. Effectively this will nullify the encroaching pull of Rugby League and star players of this tournament will not need to look to alien horizons to secure their futures. Against this setting the Rugby World Cup Final was played.

To say there was tension, fear, expectation and an almost uncanny disbelief that South Africa and New Zealand would now square off for the coveted trophy would almost be understating the fact.

Before the series started, South Africa's chances of winning were rated lower than Australia's and England's. New Zealand's were even lower. But as both teams campaigned, their strengths were evident and, as the day dawned on the highveld, New Zealand was rampantly proclaimed by experts to be the favoured team.

A state of high expectation was engendered in the capacity crowd as helicopters circled above trailing 16 nations' flags, a drummers' pageant of the nations reverberated, parachutists flew in, jets screamed in formation and SAA jumbos flew astonishingly low over the stadium.

The players came on. President Mandela shook each player's hand. National anthems were played with stirring emotion. The game was on.

There were no tries. There were no sweeping moves. Grim defence of probing offence was the watchword. Yet it was as enthralling a contest as a Fischer-Spassky chess encounter.

New Zealand made its intention clear from the first whistle. Spinning the ball at every opportunity in a bid to overwhelm South Africa with their exciting brand of "total rugby", their

MATCH 32   THE FINAL

SOUTH AFRICA	vs	NEW ZEALAND
Andre Joubert	15	Glen Osborne
James Small	14	Jeff Wilson
Japie Mulder	13	Frank Bunce
Hennie Le Roux	12	Walter Little
Chester Williams	11	Jonah Lomu
Joel Stransky	10	Andrew Mehrtens
Joost vd Westhuizen	9	Graeme Bachop
Mark Andrews	8	Zinzan Brooke
Ruben Kruger	7	Josh Kronfeld
© Francois Pienaar	6	Michael Brewer
Hannes Strydom	5	Robin Brooke
Kobus Wiese	4	Ian Jones
Balie Swart	3	Olo Brown
Chris Rossouw	2	Sean Fitzpatrick ©
Pieter du Randt	1	Craig Dowd

REFEREE : Ed Morrison (England)

Balie Swart replaced by Garry Pagel;
Mark Andrews replaced by Rudolph Straeuli;
James Small replaced by Brendan Venter

Michael Brewer replaced by Jamie Joseph;
Jeff Wilson replaced by Marc Ellis;
Craig Dowd replaced by Richard Loe.

GAME PROGRESSION
field possesion / time

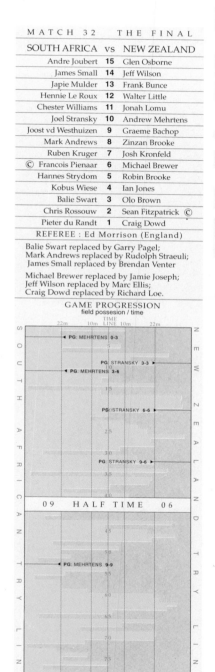

PG: MEHRTENS 0-3
PG: STRANSKY 3-3
PG: MEHRTENS 3-6
PG: STRANSKY 6-6
PG: STRANSKY 9-6
09   HALF TIME   06
PG: MEHRTENS 9-9
09   EXTRA TIME   09
PLAY CONTINUES

Captain Courageous: Francois Pienaar prepared himself and his team for the most gruelling, hard-tackling, mentally demanding match of the whole campaign, asking everything from his team and giving everything of himself.

A ticket! Any ticket! The most cherished place in South Africa on 24 June was inside Ellis Park to be among the crowd of 65 000. R200 seats were on offer at more than R2 000.

sense of adventure paid an early dividend when a lightning strike was spearheaded by Graeme Bachop, Glen Osborne, Mike Brewer and Frank Bunce. When South Africa infringed, fly-half Andrew Mehrtens made no mistake with the penalty.

First blood to the All Blacks. However, in the ensuing cut-and-thrust, the Springboks showed the first signs of the magnificent defence, tactical common sense and thunderous forward commitment that was to bring them their reward.

A half-break by fly-half Joel Stransky followed by a Mark Andrews drive saw the All Blacks offside at the ensuing ruck, Stransky levelled the account at 3 - 3.

The young New Zealand backs, staying true to coach Laurie Mains' all-action blueprint, continued to try to run the Springboks off their feet. Although Mehrtens again put them ahead after a burst up the middle by Jonah Lomu, it was clear that the All Blacks were not going to find it easy to punch holes in the South African defence.

A compelling duel developed, with the All Blacks seeking to bring their main strike weapon, Lomu, into the fray as often as possible. It was not that the slick-handling All Blacks failed to put Lomu into space, it was just that when they did, if he was not taken to task by James Small, he would find flankers Ruben Kruger or Francois Pienaar blocking his path.

South Africa's superb first-up tackling and cover defence broke up the All Blacks pattern and, consequently, the Springboks were able to mount pressure of their own. With the Bok forwards driving off the fringes, they came close to scoring the first try of the game when Kruger was judged by referee Ed Morrison to have been held up over the line. However, their efforts did not go unrewarded as Stransky slotted his second penalty and then, nine minutes before the interval, struck a sweet drop-goal to give South Africa a 9 - 6 half-time lead.

New Zealand were far from done. After the break they established territorial domination on the back of a brilliant line-out performance from the lanky Ian Jones. Throwing everything bar the kitchen sink at South Africa, they drew level with a Mehrtens drop-goal.

Then, moving into the last quarter of normal time, the game became a frenzy of action. First New Zealand, with Walter Little's pass to Lomu judged marginally forward, and then South Africa, when Joost van der Westhuizen sent Small away after a blind side break only to be called back for a

EXTRA TIME
GAME PROGRESSION
field possesion / time

PG: MEHRTENS 9-12

PG: STRANSKY 12-12

| 1 2 | H A L F   T I M E | 1 2 |

PG: STRANSKY 15-12

F I N A L   S C O R E
15 • 12

MAN OF THE MATCH: JOEL STRANSKY

S P R I N G B O K S
A L L   B L A C K S

Traditional rivals for 74 years, South Africa and New Zealand, in meeting at the Rugby World Cup Final, make this their 42nd official International.

Before the Rugby World Cup 1995 their past test record was as follows:

SOUTH AFRICA	NEW ZEALAND
TESTS WON	
20	18
TESTS DRAWN	
3	3
TOTAL POINTS SCORED	
460	430
TOTAL TRIES SCORED	
55	56
BIGGEST MARGIN	
17 - 0 Durban 1928	20 - 3 Auckland 1963
MOST INDIVIDUAL POINTS IN ONE MATCH	
20 Naas Botha Wellington 1981	18 Shane Howarth Auckland 1994

The first international was played at Carisbrook, Dunedin, 13 August 1921.

The first in South Africa was played at Kingsmead, Durban, 30 June 1928.

Graeme Bachop takes the Kiwis into a charge.
The rugby world stood in awe of Jonah Lomu. Coach Christie drilled each of his men on how to stop the man whose very name struck fear and respect into his opponents.

Glen Osborne's great effort collected no tries. Neither did anyone else's. The defences of both sides proved impenetrable.

marginally forward pass - threatened to break the deadlock.

The drama developed. Two minutes from time the All Blacks smelled victory as a Frank Bunce thrust provided a quick ruck ball, only for Mehrtens to miss a drop from in front of the posts. The final whistle went, forcing the match into extra time.

Extra time - and fate - beckoned the Springboks. With the pitch beginning to resemble a casualty ward, the first 10 minute half began well for the All Blacks, Mehrtens redeeming himself with a huge penalty.

But the Boks were not to be denied and, following a drive by Pieter du Randt, a Stransky penalty levelled the score again at 12 - 12. Then, after the break, Stransky struck gold when, from his up-and-under, South Africa were given the scrum feed on the New Zealand 22. The gifted fly-half lofted a drop goal between the uprights.

Even though he was unable to take his side six points clear with a last minute penalty, Stransky's match-winning strike was enough. South Africa's Rainbow Nation had found its pot of gold.

No-one was more overjoyed than President Nelson Mandela who, wearing a Springbok jersey, had been introduced to the two teams before the start. He trod the Ellis Park stage like a beneficent father. The seal was set on a fairy-tale tournament for South Africa by the simple exchange of words between him and captain Francois Pienaar when he presented the Webb Ellis Trophy after the game:

Mandela: *"Thank you for what you have done for South Africa."*
Pienaar: *"We could never have done what you have done for South Africa."*

Never in South Africa's history was a win more passionately wanted. Never was it delivered with more intent. Never was the sense of moment greater. Whatever the Springboks achieve in the next one hundred years, the new generations will surely look back and recall: this was their finest hour.

In every corner of the country, from the tiny settlement on the edge of the Kalahari to the boisterous, bustling Waterfront, from the isolated game reserves to the smoky heart of Soweto, the people of South Africa erupted in amazement and joy. For the first time in history they were everybody's Springboks.

They had won!

The two men who made all the difference ... Stransky takes the ball from Mehrtens.

In the end it was Man of the Match Stransky's extra kick that took the trophy.

Posters in the crowd read, "LOMU is a SMALL job", but after a great game James Small himself had problems and left the field with cramp.

Chris Rossouw leads the advance with support from Pieter du Randt and Francois Pienaar.
Mark Andrews goes high to feed the ball down to Joost van der Westhuizen.
Ruben Kruger, with Pieter du Randt and Hennie le Roux, squares up to Walter Little.

Joost van der Westhuizen flies out to the pack with a cannon ball delivery. Solid in attack and defence, his midfield tackling was a major deterrent to the looming danger of Lomu.

Andre Joubert, Rudolf Strauli and Hannes Strydom chair their captain on a slow, savouring lap of honour.

Their dream now a hard-won reality, Joost kisses the gold William Webb Ellis Trophy.

The victorious Springboks stop and acknowledge the tumultuous roar of the crowd.

From one captain to another: the golden William Webb Ellis trophy passes from President Mandela, wearing for the occasion a Springbok jersey no. 6, to the man of the occasion in jersey no. 6, Francois Pienaar.

SOUTH AFRICA 15
NEW ZEALAND 12

POOL 1

SOUTH AFRICA
AUSTRALIA
CANADA
ROMANIA

POOL 3

NEW ZEALAND
IRELAND
WALES
JAPAN

QUARTER FINAL

SOUTH AFRICA 42
WEST SAMOA 14

QUARTER FINAL

NEW ZEALAND 48
SCOTLAND 30

SEMI FINAL

SOUTH AFRICA 19
FRANCE 15

SEMI FINAL

NEW ZEALAND 45
ENGLAND 29

QUARTER FINAL

ENGLAND 25
AUSTRALIA 22

QUARTER FINAL

FRANCE 36
IRELAND 12

POOL 2

ENGLAND
WEST SAMOA
ITALY
ARGENTINA

PLAY-OFF

FRANCE 19
ENGLAND 9

POOL 4

FRANCE
SCOTLAND
TONGA
IVORY COAST

WORLD CUP RUGBY 1995

25/5	Newlands	South Africa 27 - Australia 18
26/5	Rustenburg	Scotland 89 - Ivory Coast 0
26/5	Pretoria	France 38 - Tonga 10
26/5	Port Elizabeth	Canada 34 - Romania 3
27/5	East London	West Samoa 42 - Italy 18
27/5	Bloemfontein	Wales 57 - Japan 10
27/5	Durban	England 24 - Argentina 18
27/5	Johannesburg	New Zealand 43 - Ireland 19
30/5	East London	Argentina 26 - West Samoa 32
30/5	Cape Town	South Africa 21 - Romania 8
30/5	Rustenberg	France 54 - Ivory Coast 18
30/5	Pretoria	Scotland 41 - Tonga 5
31/5	Port Elizabeth	Australia 27 - Canada 11
31/5	Bloemfontein	Ireland 50 - Japan 28
31/5	Durban	England 27 - Italy 20
31/5	Johannesburg	New Zealand 34 - Wales 9
3/6	Rustenburg	Tonga 29 - Ivory Coast 11
3/6	Stellenbosch	Australia 42 - Romania 3
3/6	Pretoria	France 22 - Scotland 19
3/6	Port Elizabeth	South Africa 20 - Canada 0
4/6	East London	Italy 31 - Argentina 25
4/6	Bloemfontein	New Zealand 145 - Japan 17
4/6	Johannesburg	Ireland 24 - Wales 23
4/6	Durban	England 44 - West Samoa 22

QUARTER-FINAL

10/6	Durban	France 36 - Ireland 12
10/6	Johannesburg	S Africa 42 - W Samoa 14
11/6	Cape Town	England 25 - Australia 22
11/6	Pretoria	NZ 48 - Scotland 30

SEMI-FINAL

| 17/6 | Durban | South Africa 19 - France 15 |
| 18/6 | Cape Town | NZ 45 - England 29 |

PLAY-OFF

| 24/6 | Pretoria | France 19 - England 9 |

THE FINAL

| 24/6 | Johannesburg | South Africa 15 - NZ 12 |

TOP TRY SCORERS IN
RUGBY WORLD CUP 1995

7	MARC ELLIS	NZL
7	JONAH LOMU	NZL
5	GAVIN HASTINGS	SCO
5	RORY UNDERWOOD	ENG
4	THIERRY LACROIX	FRA
4	ADRIAAN RICHTER	SAF
4	CHESTER WILLIAMS	SAF
3	JOSH KRONFELD	NZL
3	GARETH THOMAS	WAL
3	GEORGE HARDER	SAM
3	JOE ROFF	AUS
3	PAULO VACCARI	ITA
3	GLEN OSBORNE	NZL
3	ERIC RUSH	NZL
3	JEFF WILSON	NZL
3	PHILLIPPE SAINT ANDRE	FRA
3	TONY UNDERWOOD	ENG
3	DAMIAN SMITH	AUS
3	WALTER LITTLE	NZL

MAX BRITO

Many a hero of this Rugby World Cup has played his way into the hearts of rugby lovers, but one man, Max Brito, has touched the hearts of us all. On 3 June, playing for Ivory Coast against Tonga, his spinal cord was crushed and he was paralysed. He is living past the point that sports lovers fear most: when courage turns to calamity. Funds are being sent for his welfare but, along with this, he needs rugby friends around the world for moral support. Many feel for his plight. Few express their feeling. If you, my good reader, would like to take the initiative to send a postcard, video or message of goodwill - whenever you read this little corner of the book, now, or long into the future, his spirits will be lifted. His address is simply as follows :
MAX BRITO, BISCAROSSE, 40, FRANCE

With this book, history was in the making while history was being made. The Story of the Rugby World Cup South Africa 1995 was written, photographed and printed, section by section, as each game was played. Each story went to press leaving the last section ready for the story of the Rugby World Cup Final.

The result: 24 hours after the Webb Ellis Trophy was held aloft by the winning team, the first books were completed, bound and distributed - a record in its own right.

It is a credit to the remarkable team who, together with the speed and accuracy of state of the art technology, put this book together for your enjoyment and for rugby lovers of the world for now and for generations that will follow. This is a true collector's piece.

The concept arose from a discussion between top sports photographer John Rubython of Sports for Africa and publisher Royston Lamond. Herman van Staden and Luisa Mazinter of The Change Works, joined forces with them and made the dream a reality. WCRB, trading as 'The Book' was formed to distribute this publication. The project was financed by The Change Works and Charles Apperley and Dale Packham of Inter Africa Promotions.

The Change Works
Project Management and Marketing

The text was created principally by Paul Dobson and Nick Cain with additional copy by President Nelson Mandela, Dr Tony O'Reilly, Royston Lamond, Rodney Mazinter and Sue de Villiers. Editors were Nick Cain and Rodney Mazinter.

Special thanks go to the team who helped put this book together: Alex Kellermann, official statistician for the South African Rugby Union, for his contribution to the statistics and to Rodney Mazinter who compiled the match statistics, presented in this book in a totally new way, showing how territory was gained throughout each game, how points were scored, when and by whom. Unisys supplied computerised statistics to assist in checking data.

Statistics graphics, maps, flags, humour, Jack Daniels and page layouts by jONo

Imaging, scanning and reproduction by Frankie and Faizel of ToneGraphics.

Printed by CTP Book Printers, twice nominated Sappi Book Printers of the Year; 1993 and 1994.

PHOTOGRAPHY

Photography collated by Sport for Africa which coordinated the efforts of our international team of photographers:

Sport for Africa
John Rubython
Andrew Louwrens

The Argus
Jim McLagan
Andrew Ingram
Leon Müller
Brenton Geach
Hannes Thiart
Roy Wigley
Doug Pithey

Cape Times
Anne Laing
Alan Taylor

The Star
Etienne Rothbart
Duif du Toit

Anthony Jacobs
Pieter Els
Julius Truter
Giles Ridley
Mark van Aardt

Dave Gibson, UK
Peter Bush, New Zealand
Denys Clement, L'Equipe, Paris

Coloursport, UK
Colin Elsey

Allsport

Rugby World Cup Official Photographer
Col Whelan, Australia

Special thanks to AGFA for its support of this book from the early stages and its assistance in supplying photographic paper, film, AGFA ARCUS and STUDIO SCAN and dedicated photographic laboratory facilities at Waterfront Photo.

THE OFFICIAL COLOUR FILM SUPPLIERS OF THE RUGBY WORLD CUP 1995

It is with respect that we remember one of South Africa's leading sports writers Chris Greyvenstein who began work on this project but sadly did not live to enjoy the first game of Rugby World Cup 1995.

Special thanks to ULT which, in the space of two weeks, developed and implemented a Lotus Notes Order Entry, Production Management and Distribution System. Lotus Notes software was supplied courtesy of Lotus Development S.A. Blue Technologies supplied IBM PC workstations and a server for the production of the book.

Lotus

ERRATUM

In creating this book with a 24 hour deadline as our stated goal, some typographic errors occurred, for which the publisher apologises:

- On the page headed TONGA, the sentence should read "The Friendly Islands, some 150 of them ..." (since printing that page there are now 151, the latest volcano being named Lomu Island).
- West Samoa vs Argentina - match 9
- South Africa vs Romania - 30 May
- France vs Tonga - Pretoria
- France vs Ireland - match 24
- Chester Williams was our choice for Man of the Match for the game played on 10 June, whereas Mark Andrews was officially given the title.

Further copies of this edition are available from the publishers Royston Lamond International (Pty) Ltd, Private Bag X8, Mill Street, Cape Town, 8010. Tel: 27-21-457111 Fax: 27-21-456546

ISBN: 095839296X
CONNOISSEURS'
LEATHER BOUND EDITION

ISBN: 0958392986
HARD COVER EDITION

ISBN: 0958392978
SOFT COVER EDITION

PUBLISHED BY
ROYSTON LAMOND
INTERNATIONAL
CAPE TOWN

in association with

INDEPENDENT NEWSPAPERS HOLDINGS LIMITED

I F

If you can keep your head
    when all about you
Are losing theirs
    and blaming it on you,
If you can trust yourself
    when all men doubt you,
But make allowance
    for their doubting too;
If you can wait and
    not be tired by waiting,
Or being lied about,
    don't deal in lies,
Or being hated,
    don't give way to hating,
And yet don't look too good,
    nor talk too wise;

If you can dream - and not
    make dreams your master;
If you can think - and not
    make thoughts your aim;
If you can meet with
    Triumph and Disaster
And treat those two
    Impostors just the same.

If you can make one heap
    of all your winnings
And risk it on one turn
    of pitch-and-toss;
And lose, and start again
    at your beginnings
And never breathe a word
    about your loss.

If you can talk with crowds
    and keep your virtue,
Or walk with Kings - not lose
    the common touch,
If neither foes nor loving friends
    can hurt you,
If all men count with you,
    but none too much;

If you can fill the
    unforgiving minute
With sixty seconds' worth
    of distance run,
Yours is the Earth and
    everything that's in it,
And - which is more
    - you'll be a Man, my son!

K I P L I N G